The Effort to Save Somalia

August 1992 – March 1994

Walter S. Poole

Joint History Office
Office of the Chairman of the Joint Chiefs of Staff
Washington, DC · 2005

Foreword

Written several years after the end of operations by US forces in Somalia, this monograph focuses specifically on the involvement of the Chairman of the Joint Chiefs of Staff and the Joint Staff in planning and directing the operations in Somalia from August 1992 to March 1994. The study begins with a discussion of the conditions and circumstances that, in August 1992, led President George H. W. Bush to direct the American military to support relief efforts in Somalia and ends with the final withdrawal of US forces in 1994. The author, Dr. Walter S. Poole, relied primarily on Joint Staff files and interviews as sources of information.

In writing this account, Dr. Poole was given valuable help by many of the key participants and members of the Joint Staff; their contributions are cited in the footnotes. The final manuscript was reviewed by Dr. Poole and edited by Dr. David A. Armstrong; Ms. Susan Carroll prepared the index and Ms. Penny Norman prepared the manuscript for publication.

This study was reviewed for declassification by the appropriate US Government agencies and cleared for release. The volume is an official publication of the Office of the Chairman of the Joint Chiefs of Staff, but the views expressed are those of the author and do not represent the official position of the Chairman or the Joint Chiefs of Staff.

David A. Armstrong
Director for Joint History

Washington, DC
August 2005

Contents

Overview

In shaping policy towards Somalia, the Chairman of the Joint Chiefs of Staff, the Vice Chairman, and the Joint Staff had to advise how US military forces could execute an evolving range of missions "other than war": humanitarian relief and suppression of banditry, followed by peace enforcement with international forces under United Nations (UN) command, all accompanied by a nation-building effort. The experience of the Vietnam War, where US military involvement deepened while political goals remained misty, shaped their thinking. From the beginning, these officers sought a definition of the political goals or "end-state" in Somalia. Yet, despite their efforts, US objectives underwent repeated change.

Press images of a massive famine provoked US intervention in Somalia. Severe drought destroyed local crops and famine resulted when marauding gangs seized food and blocked the distribution of relief supplies. Minimizing risks for US forces by confining them to ensuring the flow of aid also meant minimizing their role in political reconciliation and reconstruction. On the other hand, widening US military missions could further the attainment of political objectives but risked American casualties. Such losses eventually did turn public opinion against continued US involvement there.

In August 1992, as C-130s began an airlift of relief supplies, the Joint Staff warned about the danger of being drawn into an open-ended commitment. The State Department, on the other hand, recommended committing US ground troops to guard food distribution facilities at "points of security." The Joint Staff warned against such a "long-term commitment of resources in a no-win situation," and the Deputies Committee (DC) of the National Security Council (NSC) chose to seek UN forces for such tasks. During Deputies Committee meetings, the Vice Chairman, Admiral David E. Jeremiah, sought a definition of the Bush administration's political objective or "end-point" in Somalia. Meanwhile, graphic media accounts of mass starvation drove policy. Late in November, with relief efforts hamstrung by feuding warlords, the dispatch of US ground troops to assure the distribution of relief supplies became a serious option. The Joint Staff wanted to keep the US role minimal and allow the UN contingents to play a more active role. But Jeremiah and the Chairman, General Colin L. Powell, USA, reluctantly concluded that matters had deteriorated to the point where nothing except large-scale ground intervention in Somalia would work. President George H. W. Bush directed that course of action. But, as General Powell and Secretary of Defense Dick (Richard) Cheney warned, the outgoing administration's goal of withdrawing US forces by 20 January 1993 proved unattainable.

Even before the first US troops landed in Mogadishu on 9 December, Chairman Powell and the Commander in Chief, US Central Command, (USCINC-CENT), General Joseph Hoar, USMC, sought to limit their mission, withdraw combat units as soon as possible, and quickly transfer responsibility from the US-led Unified Task Force (UNITAF) to the UN-led Operation in Somalia (UNOSOM). Although UN Secretary General Boutros Boutros-Ghali wanted UNITAF to disarm all factions throughout the country, Powell and Hoar ensured that UNITAF remained focused on its humanitarian mission. Disarmament was enforced simply to the extent that, within UNITAF's area of operations, heavy weapons were permitted only in small, clearly defined cantonment areas. The US military opposed having UNITAF completely disarm the population. This undertaking appeared totally unrealistic because a Somali clan felt safe only if its members were heavily armed.

The efforts of UNITAF could be rated a success in the sense that, when UNOSOM took over on 4 May 1993, Mogadishu was calm, heavy weapons had been stored in cantonments, and marauding gangs were suppressed. Food supplies were flowing, starvation practically had ceased, drought eased, and seeds and livestock were being replenished. The clans still had their customary arsenals of small arms, however, and the warlords showed little willingness to compromise or negotiate in good faith.

General Powell, Admiral Jeremiah and the Joint Staff argued that since humanitarian, political and security goals were so interdependent, an integrated US and UN policy must be established. Progress had to occur concurrently along all the tracks of this three-track strategy. Without a stable government, functioning police forces, and long-term economic aid, Somalia would slide back toward disaster. As matters turned out, the humanitarian task was accomplished, but security steadily eroded and political reconstruction was stillborn.

In June 1993, after Mohammed Farah Aideed's militiamen killed twenty-four Pakistani troops, Pakistan's representative on the Security Council demanded a prompt and strong UN response. The Joint Staff reviewed a series of drafts from the

UN and the NSC Staff; General Powell and Admiral Jeremiah were consulted about wording, but they neither saw the final text nor knew that it had been approved at the White House. The result, Resolution 837, authorized "all necessary measures" to arrest and detain those who had either incited or carried out the attack. This commitment was hastily made, yet it had consequences that drew the United States directly into Somalia's civil war. The administration wanted UNOSOM to succeed without US forces playing a prominent role. UNOSOM, however, inherited a shrunken UNITAF at the time of the turnover, and was controlled by a headquarters initially manned at only twenty-two percent of its authorized strength. UNOSOM's civil and political elements also had significant shortfalls in staffing. Furthermore, a US quick reaction force (QRF) constituted UNOSOM's teeth and US logistic support units made up its tail. The UNOSOM headquarters often used the QRF for dangerous missions while many other national contingents either served in the much more stable countryside or stayed in garrison in Mogadishu.

The UN Special Representative, Admiral Jonathan T. Howe, USN (Ret), who had been President Bush's Deputy National Security Adviser, pressed forcefully and repeatedly for deploying US Special Operations Forces (SOF) to capture Aideed. By issuing an arrest warrant for Aideed and then offering a reward, Howe made that warlord the focus of US and UN attention. The State Department and the NSC staff agreed with Howe that removing Aideed would make "all the difference." However, the Joint Staff, early in July, recommended limiting our efforts to "marginalizing" Aideed on grounds that sending the SOF would turn the "UN versus Aideed" battle into a "US versus Aideed" confrontation. The Director, J-5, Lieutenant General Barry McCaffrey, USA, conversely, supported sending SOF if USCINCCENT and the commanders on the ground wanted them. Late in July, an interagency team with Joint Staff representation visited Mogadishu and recommended making SOF available. General Powell, however, continued to oppose sending SOF because, like General Hoar, he saw many dangers and little hope of success.

In policy deliberations, the Deputies Committee wavered; finally, in mid-August, it moved toward the State-NSC approach of removing Aideed. On 21 August, after ambushes of US troops and at the request of General Hoar, General Powell reluctantly changed his mind and recommended deploying SOF. Secretary of Defense Les Aspin approved sending a 440-man task force. A month later, as clashes continued and Aideed eluded capture, the Deputies Committee considered re-energizing the political track and simply isolating Aideed, perhaps even reaching an accommodation with him. Secretary of Defense Aspin spoke of devising an "exit strategy" from Somalia; the Joint Staff also started working out a course of action. But policy adjustments by the Deputies Committee were so finely nuanced that lower echelons did not interpret them as major changes and field commanders could not translate them into concrete actions. The SOF pursued the military track by hunting Aideed even as General Hoar limited the QRF's role to "force protection" and Secretary Aspin rejected a military request for a small number of tanks and Infantry Fighting Vehicles (IFV) to strengthen the QRF. On 30 September, his last day in office, the Chairman advised President Clinton that the situation in Somalia was unraveling and all US and UN troops should be withdrawn. The policy muddle was exposed by a battle three days later that left eighteen US soldiers dead and turned the administration toward a speedy withdrawal of US troops.

Two years after the effort to save Somalia began, events there seemed to have circled back toward anarchy and clan warfare. Success in humanitarian relief was not followed by nation-building because the underlying political and security problems were never solved. The UN proved woefully inadequate for the latter tasks, with operations in the field and in New York hobbled by inertia, undermanning and incompetence. Shortcomings in US policy-making contributed to the unsatisfactory outcome. Somalia was a frequent topic of discussion among the President and his senior advisors, but for the months between November 1992 when President Bush decided to intervene and October 1993 when President Clinton decided to pull out, discussions in the Deputies Committee where policy alternatives were formulated usually revolved around short-term tactics without reference to long-term objectives. Imprecision and drift often seemed to reign. Steps that General Hoar condemned as "mission creep" depended upon how the mission was being defined at that moment. Those who favored deploying SOF relied upon the maxim of fighting to win. Lieutenant General McCaffrey, the J-5, spoke of targeting Aideed without "personalizing" the conflict but did not specify how this would be avoided. General Powell wanted to keep objectives limited, which meant minimizing US military involvement. His change of mind about using SOF came in response to ambushes of US troops, not as part of a broad policy reconsideration. Within a few weeks after the SOF reached Mogadishu, the Deputies Committee began swinging back toward an accommodation with Aideed. Yet every change of tactics seemed only to reduce policymakers' maneuver room and make UNOSOM's success less likely. The hunt for Aideed continued, culminating in the firefight of 3 October. After that battle, the White House decided that any option other than prompt withdrawal had become unattainable.

Chapter 1
UNOSOM I: First Efforts Falter

The US experience in Somalia has proven unique for two reasons. First, intervention sprang entirely from the humanitarian motive of saving lives. In a land ravaged by famine, the aim was to avert mass starvation by ending anarchy and permitting relief supplies to flow again. As news stories from Somalia grew relentlessly more grim, the Chairman of the Joint Chiefs of Staff, the Vice Chairman, and Joint Staff officers confronted the question of whether and how to use military force in a situation that threatened no US security interests and met none of the historic criteria for intervention. What, they asked, was the objective or "end state" to be sought? Their experiences made them keen to avoid a situation where military commitments would mount while political goals remained misty. Nonetheless, US objectives in Somalia underwent constant change. Second, an international force under a United Nations command tried to keep the peace, impose reconciliation upon warring Somali factions, and assist in rebuilding governmental institutions. Here the Chairman, Vice Chairman and Joint Staff had to cope with the shortcomings of an operation that was being managed not only by UN headquarters in New York but also by dozens of contributing governments. Too often, satisfactory solutions could not be found. The US experience in Somalia raised serious questions about whether politico-military goals could be integrated with a humanitarian mission and about the viability of peace enforcement operations under UN direction.

The Road to Tragedy

Somalia became an independent nation in 1960, but its political tradition of shifting alliances among clans and sub-clans fitted poorly with parliamentary government and free elections. In 1969, General Mohammed Siad Barre seized power. In 1977, he invaded the Ogaden region of neighboring Ethiopia, which was populated largely by ethnic Somalis. Almost simultaneously, Barre broke military ties with the USSR and obtained military equipment from the United States, the United Kingdom and France. The Soviets reacted by rushing arms, advisers and Cuban troops to Ethiopia; Barre's troops were trounced and driven back into Somalia. Although he stayed in power, opposition to Barre's rule mounted steadily. A full-scale guerrilla war began in May 1988. Barre's soldiers retaliated by killing tens of thousands of civilians, but repression only made the opposition stronger. On 27 January 1991, after four weeks of fighting that devastated the capital city of Mogadishu and compelled the evacuation of US Embassy personnel by helicopter, Barre fled south. Much of the country's infrastructure lay in ruins. Perhaps what had passed for the normality of a nation-state in Somalia was really an aberration, created and financed by Cold War rivalry.[1]

Clan and sub-clan warfare spread across Somalia. In the north, a breakaway Somaliland Republic came into being. Partisans of "provisional president" Ali Mahdi and clansmen of General Mohammed Aideed fought each other in Mogadishu. Barre's son-in-law, General Hersi Morgan, led fighters in the south; his main rival was Omar Jess. Arms were readily available to all factions, with weapons worth $9 billion coming from the USSR between 1975 and 1989, and another $4 billion in arms coming from eighteen countries, including the United States and Libya, between 1985 and 1989. Moreover, after the overthrow of Haile Mariam Mengistu in Ethiopia, many of Mengistu's soldiers returned to their villages and sold their weapons to Somalis at bargain prices.

Launching the Airlift

Somalia as a nation and as a cohesive society had dissolved. Then an unusually severe drought struck. Food became a form of currency and marauding gangs seized this "money." In mid-December 1991, the first relief supplies from abroad reached war-torn Mogadishu. Within thirty days, however, the International Committee of the Red Cross (ICRC) warned that starvation threatened hundreds of thousands of refugees living in camps south of the capital. On 23 January 1992, the UN Security Council urged all parties to accept a cease-fire and urged states to contribute to humanitarian assistance. Three months later, the Council approved Resolution 751 (1) requesting Secretary General Boutros Boutros-Ghali to send fifty observers who would monitor a very fragile cease-fire in Mogadishu and (2) agreeing in principle to establish a UN security force for Somalia when the necessary conditions existed. The first UN observers arrived on 23 July. Simultaneously, UN Special Representative Mohammed Sahnoun estimated that 1.5 million Somalis faced imminent starvation. Private humanitarian organizations launched a worldwide appeal for aid.

The US government, which would have to pay for thirty-one percent of any UN peacekeeping operation, did not want to find itself funding "food guards" and hoped that voluntary contributions from Saudi Arabia and other neighbors would suffice. But late in July 1992, as pictures of skeletal children jolted the American public, President George H. W. Bush decided that the United States should play a leading, visible role. That meant accelerating deliveries of food and medicine, promoting reconciliation among clans and warlords, and funding the deployment of UN food guards. An interagency Somalia Working Group, organized at White House direction, met for the first time on 30 July. Its chairman, Deputy Assistant Secretary of State Robert Houdek, asked the Joint Staff to estimate the costs of air-dropping, airlifting or heli-lifting relief supplies.[2]

In the Joint Staff, the principal action officers for the first round of support to Somalia were Lieutenant Colonels John Wahlquist, USAF, and (as of 1 October) Perry Baltimore, USA, in J-5's Middle East-Africa Division (MEAF), Lieutenant Colonels David Van Esselstyn, USMC, and Frank Brittain, USA, in J-3's Joint Operations Division (JOD), and Lieutenant Colonel John Newton, USAF, in the J-4 Logistic Readiness Center (LRC). One or more of these officers would attend interagency Working Group meetings. Often, Wahlquist and Baltimore drafted the position papers that went to the Chairman. At the next level, Rear Admiral Frank P. Bowman, Assistant Deputy Director for Politico-Military Affairs, J-5, usually attended Somalia sessions of the Policy Coordinating Committee (PCC). Admiral David E. Jeremiah, the Vice Chairman, served as JCS representative on the National Security Council Deputies Committee; Bowman often accompanied him.

Although President Bush kept himself informed, NSC Principals did not meet about Somalia until late November when a major decision had to be made. By then, incremental decisions below that level had led the administration toward intervention. This pattern of policy choices being debated and determined below the Principals' level would remain consistent during most of the American involvement in Somalia.

In mid-1992, the Office of the Secretary of Defense (OSD) possessed more expertise about Somalia than the Joint Staff. However, Deputy Assistant Secretary James Woods struck some officers in J-5 MEAF as overly enthusiastic about US involvement there. MEAF officers also regarded their State Department counterparts with caution. The Joint Staff's attitude toward involvement in Somalia was one of extreme wariness. An appraisal by Smith Hempstone, a conservative journalist with extensive African experience who was US ambassador to neighboring Kenya, mirrored action officers' convictions so accurately that it would be quoted or paraphrased in a number of Joint Staff papers:

There is little reason to believe that the bitter and long-standing clan rivalries that have turned Somalia into a particularly murderous African Lebanon will yield to outside intervention.... Tragic as the situation is in Somalia ... the dissolution of the Somali nation-state does not affect vital USG security interests. Accordingly, USG should think—and think again—before allowing itself to become bogged down in a quagmire without the promise of offsetting concomitant benefits.[3]

On 4 August, the Director, J-4, sent OSD an estimate of the costs of using two C-130 aircraft and three CH-47 helicopters for sixty days of delivering relief supplies. The Defense Department would have to spend about $3 million for the C-130s alone, about $7 million for the C-130s and CH-47s. The J-4 urged, however, that the administration approach this mission "with *extreme caution*" and paraphrased Ambassador Hempstone's appraisal: "The sad fact is that no outside intervention can prevent a people intent on destroying themselves from succeeding if they so insist."[4]

When the Somalia Working Group met again on 5 August, a spokesman from the Agency for International Development's (AID) Office of Foreign Disaster Assistance proposed funding Red Cross flights into Somalia and limiting the military airlift to flights from Nairobi or Mombasa to Wajir, Kenya, near the Somali border. The Wajir airfield lay close to a refugee center established by the Kenyan government. In that case, commented Lieutenant Colonel Van Esselstyn, truck convoys would be cheaper and more efficient. Likewise, J-5 officers deemed a military airlift unwarranted and undesirable.[5]

Political and humanitarian concerns overrode the Joint Staff's objections. On 4 August, UN Special Representative Sahnoun had reported that 1.5 million Somalis would be at risk of starvation within a few weeks; hundreds were believed to be dying every day. Eight days later, Secretary General Boutros-Ghali announced that five hundred Pakistanis would go to Somalia as security guards for relief supplies. This force was christened United Nations Operation in Somalia (UNOSOM). President Bush promptly decided that US military aircraft would help transport the Pakistanis.

The Policy Coordinating Committee, chaired by Assistant Secretary of State for African Affairs Herman Cohen, met on 12 August. An NSC spokesman said that the White House wanted to be seen as taking a leading role in relief efforts.

Mr. Robert Wolthuis, Deputy Assistant Secretary of Defense (Global Affairs), reminded conferees that Operation PROVIDE COMFORT aiding the Kurds in northern Iraq, already had taken more than $1 billion from Defense's budget. But every time the conferees started talking about specifics and limitations upon Defense assets, Cohen would interrupt: "Remember, people are dying." Afterwards, Mr. Wolthuis told Joint Staff representatives that something would be done; the only question was how much.[6] Very soon afterward, the State Department circulated a paper that mentioned such options as seizing and operating a command and control facility in Mogadishu as well as establishing a UN headquarters for heavy airlift operations. J-5 MEAF officers opposed these proposals.[7]

In preparation for an NSC Deputies Committee meeting on 14 August, MEAF officers drafted a paper intended to emphasize the perils of intervention. It cautioned that, although the United States had no vital interests in Somalia, the world community felt that Washington had a moral commitment because of US security assistance given to Somalia during the Cold War. Officers in J-5, MEAF, expressed concern that by agreeing to fly the five hundred Pakistanis into Mogadishu, the administration had "signed a blank check" to commit more resources. A UN Security Council resolution authorizing "all necessary measures" to secure Mogadishu airfield was under consideration. But such a resolution could create an open-ended commitment and set a dangerous precedent. The security situation at the airfield was unclear, and the Joint Staff worried about having to insert "peacekeepers" by force. Although other agencies were discussing US military intervention, either unilaterally or under UN auspices, no clear objectives had been defined and an intruding force would face major challenges. The author of the paper closed by quoting portions of Ambassador Hempstone's bleak appraisal.[8]

The Deputies Committee, on 14 August, agreed that Defense would carry out an emergency food airlift, not only from Mombasa to Wajir but also to towns within Somalia as soon as security and operating conditions permitted. After sixty days, if feasible, military transports would be replaced by commercial or contract aircraft. President Bush publicly announced the plan for an airlift that same day. Andrew Natsios became Special Coordinator for aid to Somalia, an undertaking that now bore the name Operation PROVIDE RELIEF.[9]

On 15 August, General Powell sent an alert order to the Commander in Chief, Central Command, (USCINCCENT), General Joseph P. Hoar, USMC; an execute order to start the airlift followed next day. At the outset, four C-141s and eight C-130 aircraft were committed to supporting PROVIDE RELIEF. Two C-130s arrived at Wajir on 21 August; four C-130s made the first US military flight into Belet Uen, Somalia, seven days later.[10]

Debating "Points of Security"

Aircraft brought food to distribution points in Somalia; looters and armed thugs then seized it. Non-governmental relief organizations shipped in supplies, but food was being stolen as soon as it reached the docks. Nonetheless, warehouses still held a good deal of food; freeing and distributing these stores was the problem.

Clearly, starvation would continue unless anarchy and banditry were quelled. Truck convoys appeared to be the only way to distribute and deliver enough tonnage. Accordingly, State and the Agency for International Development's (AID) Office of Foreign Disaster Assistance (OFDA) pressed for establishing "points of security" or "zones of tranquility." Under this approach, US ground troops would guard such critical facilities as airports, feeding centers and key roads. In a paper written for Admiral Jeremiah, MEAF officers argued against adopting State's concept. Without a much larger commitment of combat force, they noted, it would be very difficult and costly to create an environment like that in Operation *Provide Comfort*, which involved feeding and protecting the Kurds in northern Iraq. By pursuing an interventionist policy in Somalia, J-5 action officers correctly forecast, "we set ourselves up for a long-term commitment of resources in a no-win situation." The longer US operations in Somalia continued, the less incentive there would be for the UN to implement its own program. However, on 20 August, the Deputies Committee agreed to develop further the "points of security" concept, pursue an "all necessary measures" resolution in the Security Council, expedite the movement of five hundred Pakistanis, and coordinate relief shipments with private and multilateral organizations.[11]

On 24 August, after hearing a UN technical team's report, Secretary General Boutros-Ghali proposed deploying 750 UN soldiers to each of four security zones within Somalia. Counting the five hundred Pakistanis, UN security forces would total thirty-five hundred. Four days later, through Resolution 775, the Security Council approved his proposal.

The Policy Coordinating Committee met on 1 September, with Rear Admiral Bowman attending. The US airlift was going well and soon would reach a level of fourteen C-130s; it also would be expanded to cover towns where clan leaders exercised control and security risks remained low. Reporting on his recent trip to Kenya and Somalia, Mr. Andrew Natsios of AID said that the UN relief effort labored under serious operational and organizational handicaps. But he recommended putting "points of security" under UN auspices, without involving US troops. Most conferees, including Bowman, agreed that implementing "points of security" as a US effort would be premature and would conflict with the aim of having the UN take responsibility for guarding relief supplies. On 4 September, the Deputies Committee endorsed establishing "points of security" under UN auspices. The idea then was presented to Marrack Goulding, Under Secretary General for Peacekeeping Operations, who appeared receptive.[12]

"Points of security," however, proved hard to find. On 5 September, C-130s from Kenya began delivering supplies to Baidoa. Nine days later, C-5A and C-141 aircraft landed the first Pakistani soldiers at Mogadishu. An Amphibious Ready Group (ARG) carrying about two thousand Marines had taken up station twenty-five nautical miles off Mogadishu. But the Pakistanis, outgunned by the warlords, did not try to move out from the airfield and could not be persuaded to protect relief convoys. At Baidoa and Belet Uen, as soon as food appeared, armed gangs as well as starving people migrated to those towns. The resulting turmoil led to a temporary suspension of US relief flights. When food ran out, the gangs would leave those towns and refugees again would be left to starve.[13]

Back in early August, the cost of a sixty-day airlift had been calculated at $9.5 million. The NSC had decided that Defense would pay $8 million and State $1.5 million. By mid-September, it appeared that sixty-day costs would balloon to $30 million.[14] When the PCC reconvened on 23 September, members discussed how soon relief deliveries could shift from military to civilian aircraft. Congress and the Pentagon were getting complaints from civilian carriers who operated in Africa and wanted a share of work. The most realistic scenario, the PCC agreed, assumed that road corridors would open late in November following the deployment of UN security forces. All representatives then approved the following timetable: operate fourteen C-130s until 1 October, ten from 1-15 October, and four from 15 October until 30 November. The cost would be $24 million to Defense, $12 million to State and AID.[15]

During 23-24 September, Admiral Jeremiah visited Kenya and stopped briefly at Oddur in Somalia. He then advised General Powell that, although the UN effort fell short in manning and equipment, an adequate force could accomplish the task with relatively little risk. Outside Mogadishu, the security problem consisted of "technicals" (pickup trucks with automatic weapons mounted on them) and marauding teenagers, none a match for organized ground troops.

At a Deputies Committee meeting on 28 September, Under Secretary of State Frank Wisner gave a pessimistic appraisal of UN plans to deploy more troops and of the prospects for inter-clan political negotiations. Admiral Jeremiah recommended keeping fourteen C-130s flying for another two weeks. Admiral Jonathan Howe, USN, (Ret), Deputy Assistant to the President for National Security Affairs, agreed to do so. Deliveries, Howe emphasized, had to remain at current levels throughout the transition to a civilian airlift. Conferees approved, in principle, ending the military airlift on 1 December. They thought that relief should be changing from air to ground delivery but were unclear whether the UN had come to grips with the role its contingents would play in ensuring the safety of ground convoys. Admiral Howe also established, under the leadership of the Assistant Secretary of Defense for International Security Affairs (ISA), an interagency planning group to consider what "points of security" would require. The Joint Staff had voiced reservations about creating such a group, fearing that it might push for deploying US troops to "points of security." Admiral Jeremiah observed that the administration needed to define the "end-point" of US policy, particularly as regards political objectives. At his direction, in mid-October, MEAF officers drew up a "PERT (Program Evaluation and Review Techniques) chart" (page 101) that outlined a series of sequential goals under three categories—humanitarian, security, and political—leading to the end-states of self-sufficiency, stability and reconciliation. A PERT chart breaks down an undertaking into its component activities, puts the relationships among various activities into networks, and establishes time estimates for completing the networks as well as the total project. Regularly updated and displayed at interagency discussions, the chart tracked progress in each category and showed how the goals in the three categories were interrelated.[16]

During October, however, the "end-point" of US policy continued to elude definition. From Kenya, Ambassador Hempstone advocated ending Operation *Provide Relief*, at least in its current form, on 30 October: "Now is the time to declare victory in Somalia and go home, if only to regroup for other missions." The new interagency planning group studied what forces were required to protect relief supplies from their arrival in Mogadishu to their delivery in Baidoa and outlying areas. The group concluded that a brigade-size task force of about three thousand personnel would be needed. When these numbers were presented to the PCC on 9 October, LTC Baltimore sensed that members were surprised by how large they were. "I believe it opened some eyes," he reported to J-5. The PCC decided against submitting this case study to the UN, lest it be interpreted as indicating US willingness to fund such an undertaking. The PCC also proposed sending the last C-130 home on 15 December. Mr. Natsios strongly dissented, claiming that C-130s represented a visible US presence that charter or civilian aircraft could not duplicate. In rebuttal, members said that the military had other missions, and that a political message could be conveyed by various means.[17]

The Deputies Committee, on 21 October, endorsed efforts to encourage a greater UN security presence. It approved ending the military airlift on either 15 December or 25 January. After that meeting, the Chairman agreed to 25 January. But worsening conditions within Somalia soon made these steps seem inadequate. In Mogadishu, Aideed refused to let the five hundred Pakistanis protect the airport, the docks or food convoys. UN Special Envoy Sahnoun resigned on 26 October, after publicly criticizing the inadequacy of relief efforts. Two days later, Secretary General Boutros-Ghali asked the United States to air and sealift the three thousand troops authorized by Security Council Resolution 775: one battalion each from Belgium, Canada, Egypt and Nigeria, a Norwegian headquarters company, and a Pakistani augmentation. Apparently, Boutros-Ghali hoped that initiating air and sea movements would spur the warlords to bow to world opinion and not block these new contingents.[18]

On 2 November, Rear Admiral Bowman talked to Brigadier General Baril, the Secretary General's Military Adviser. Baril said that UN troops would enter Somalia only with the consent of the parties, since this was to be a peacekeeping rather than a peace enforcement operation. All deployments had been suspended until Sahnoun's successor, Ismet Kittani, could make an on-scene assessment.[19]

The National Security Council, on 4 November, agreed in principle to transport UN troops, if the security environment was "permissive." The State Department and the Joint Staff had opposed going even that far. Repeated UN appeals for free lift were not well received in the Joint Staff. Defense, with Admiral Jeremiah's concurrence, now relented on condition that State would bear fifty percent of the cost, estimated to total $23 million.[20]

Chapter 2
UNITAF Halts the Anarchy

Ball Peen or Sledge Hammer?

When the PCC reconvened on 6 November, members were in a somber mood. The Chairman, Deputy Assistant Secretary Robert Houdek, asked the Central Intelligence Agency to assess whether the UN's strategy appeared likely to succeed. Three days later Intelligence Community analysts conducted a video-teleconference (VTC) in which officers from J-3, J-4 and J-5 participated. The consensus was that far more than thirty-five hundred troops would be needed to ensure that relief supplies reached the two million Somalis in danger of starvation. Once UN troops were inserted, moreover, tremendous logistical difficulties would arise in maintaining them. Lieutenant Colonel Robert Bray, USA, Joint Operations Division, J-3, analyzed "points of security" requirements for Bardera, where a five hundred-man Belgian battalion had been designated as the UN peacekeeping force. He concluded that, because the battalion would have to concentrate all its assets in order to conduct one escort mission, the force's strength should be raised to between seventeen hundred and two thousand personnel.[1]

Meanwhile in Mogadishu, Aideed continued to threaten the five hundred Pakistanis and block the unloading of relief supplies. Richard Clarke of the NSC Staff asked whether the Joint Staff was doing evacuation planning. "No," was the reply; the objective should be finding ways to make the Pakistanis more effective. From UN headquarters in New York, on 6 November, US Ambassador Edward Perkins sent the State Department his judgment that the worldwide credibility of UN peacekeeping efforts was at stake. The Serbs in Bosnia and the Khmer Rouge in Cambodia would pay no heed to the Security Council "if bandits force it to take flight in Somalia." Consequently, he pressed for "a clear show of force and a demonstrable willingness to use it" against "the smallest bully on the block." Also during this time, Senegal was organizing an African push for a UN-sponsored trusteeship for Somalia. The massive unknowns of that course, Perkins argued, created a good case for trying harder to make the current effort succeed. His cable would be quoted frequently at interagency discussions.[2]

General Hoar was asked to assess Ambassador Perkins' report; he did not submit a written reply, due to his concern that it might find its way into the inter-agency arena and be misinterpreted. Instead, CENTCOM planners orally provided the Joint Staff with two options. First, station a Marine Amphibious Ready Group (MARG) off the coast; it would be able to evacuate the Pakistanis but not secure Mogadishu. (On 10 November, the Pakistanis finally took control of the airport and set up a perimeter.) Second, deploy a carrier battle group off the coast. To force a lodgment ashore, either a reinforced MARG or an Army mechanized infantry brigade would be required.

Hoar worried that, if the United States took the lead, other nations would not join what they perceived to be unilateral action. The UN first should develop a detailed plan; then the United States could decide what role to play. Colonel Frank W. Brittain, USA, of J-3 informed his superiors that he favored deploying a carrier battle group, because doing so would force the UN to make a choice while avoiding any commitment of US ground troops.[3]

The PCC, on 12 November, endorsed the intelligence community's pessimistic assessment and agreed that the Deputies Committee must decide whether to recommend a significantly larger UN troop presence. To make matters worse, it was becoming clear that the airlift alone could not avert mass starvation. Moreover, airlift costs for FY 1993 probably would exceed $60 million; AID could not pay for civilian planes to move the same tonnage currently being delivered by military aircraft. Consequently, Mr. Natsios stressed that the AID-funded airlift would drop from seven to two planes on 25 February, one month after the military airlift ended. Obviously, only a great increase in surface transport could offset this loss; there was little prospect of that. On 16 November, Special Representative Kittani reported that humanitarian supplies had become the basis of an otherwise non-existent economy. Somali "authorities" at all levels competed for anything of value; threats and killings often decided the outcome. Large sums were being extorted from private relief agencies; perhaps no more than twenty percent of relief supplies actually reached the needy. In Mogadishu, where the five hundred lightly-armed Pakistanis still were virtual hostages of the warlords, the airport had come under heavy fire on 13 November and "provisional president" Mahdi's men prevented ships from docking.[4]

Chaos of a purely bureaucratic kind reigned in New York. Ambassador Perkins, on 17 November, provided the State Department with a graphic picture of the confusion within the UN Secretariat. The Belgians' deployment planned for Bardera had been changed to Kismayo and then, partly because General Hersi

Morgan's men were advancing toward Kismayo, changed again to Mogadishu in support of the Pakistanis. Egyptian peacemakers might prove unacceptable anywhere in Somalia. Months might pass before Nigerians were ready for any deployment. The last time the Nigerians prepared to deploy, their provisions had included a herd of cattle and several hundred chickens. "Simply stated," said the Ambassador, "nobody has a clear idea who will be deployed, what they will take, where they will go, or when they will arrive."[5]

On 19 November, Under Secretary Wisner asked Secretary General Boutros-Ghali what the United States could do and what kind of help would be most effective. Boutros-Ghali, perhaps believing that the administration sought an invitation to act militarily, "stated emphatically that such assistance would not be helpful."[6]

After a Deputies Committee meeting on 20 November, the J-3 drafted a warning order requesting USCINCCENT to list courses of action that involved deploying US combat troops to major ports and to relief centers in Somalia's interior. Two days later, General Hoar proposed three alternatives:

1. At Kismayo in the south, a brigade-size force would establish a lodgement area. During its later phases, the operation would expand to Mogadishu.

2. A division-size force would secure Mogadishu. Movement to Kismayo and into the interior would occur during later phases.

3. Mogadishu and Kismayo would be seized simultaneously.

Hoar recommended the second alternative because it focused on Somalia's political center of gravity and seized the largest port early; but he also rated alternative 1 an acceptable course.[7]

The administration now had to decide whether to commit combat troops and in what strength. Ambassador Hempstone, on 20 November, argued for using US ground troops strictly as food guards and buffer forces in supporting traditional clan boundaries, without challenging the warlords. Hempstone thought that American occupation of Somalia would prove roughly comparable to Syria's position in Lebanon. Syrians exercised operational control there and had imposed a semblance of order but lacked real legitimacy so that, if they left, a rapid breakdown would follow. The difference with Somalia, he claimed, was that the Syrians "want Lebanon and are willing to pay the price of occupying it."[8]

In fact, J-5 MEAF action officers had developed three broad options, only one of which mentioned ground troops. These were:

Option 1: Continue the current course, although with more US air and sealift.

Option 2, which was favored by the State Department: Push the UN to move more quickly and commit more troops (10,000 to 15,000 instead of 3,500). The United States would provide logistical support units and deploy a Marine Amphibious Ready Group to deter Somali attacks upon UN forces.

Option 3: Organize under UN auspices a US-led coalition, equal to a division in strength and containing US ground forces.[9]

On 23 November, the Deputies Committee considered these options. They discussed ways by which US officers might continue commanding US troops under a camouflage of UN control. Conferees looked upon the Korean War, when the Security Council authorized the US Government to appoint a commander, as a good precedent. The other major issue involved whether US troops should focus upon starvation relief and let the UN deal with political issues. Military spokesmen did not believe that such a distinction was possible and called attention to interrelationships traced by the PERT chart. Mogadishu and Kismayo were only the initial military objectives. Troops would have to move into the hinterlands later, challenging the warlords and thus destabilizing the political situation. Therefore, they held, performing relief missions also meant pursuing structural political changes. The President needed to know about the political side as well as the military one. He also should be made aware that a timetable of four to six months was meaningless; events would determine the pace of progress and withdrawal. All the conferees agreed that thirty-five hundred UN troops were too few and that about fifteen thousand would be needed.[10]

On 24 November, working under Rear Admiral Bowman's supervision, Wahlquist and Baltimore prepared a talking paper for Admiral Jeremiah. Under all options, their paper stated, a sizeable peacemaking force (either UN or a UN-sanctioned coalition) would establish a food distribution system, then be replaced by a smaller peacekeeping force. The paper held that Option 1 (the current course) did not go far enough and failed to demonstrate US resolve, particularly in a "non-permissive" environment. Option 2 (10-15,000 troops) would mean committing about three thousand US medical, transport, quartermaster, intelligence and engineer troops. It was conceptually sound but unlikely to come about because other countries probably would not contribute significant combat forces unless the United States did. Option 3 (a division-size force) appeared "promising, doable, and could be quick," especially if the United States provided the bulk of forces. But it would impose a US solution and could cost billions, risk American lives and likely lead to a very long-term commitment. Such action, moreover, could set a precedent for demands for US leadership throughout Africa. There also was a potential public relations problem to consider—killing teenage bandits to save starving children will not sell well on CNN. Beyond that, Option 3 understated by a factor of three or four the size of the force required. (A revision of 25 November changed that factor to two or three—"more like 32,000.")

Thus, in summation, an invasion of Somalia would be overkill. Diplomatic efforts had not been exhausted; conditions remained dire in Mogadishu but showed improvement in the interior. Somalia's warlords should be sent a message "using the ball peen, not the sledge." Specifically, the ball peen would strike with more strength than Option 1 but less than Option 2, positioning a MARG offshore and concentrating ground contingents in Mogadishu with or without the agreement of local factions. If this approach failed, preparations should be made to launch Option 3 after President-elect Clinton had been inaugurated.[11]

When the Deputies Committee convened later that day, 24 November, some members argued that the factions must be disarmed before mostly US peacemakers could be replaced by UN peacekeepers. Military representatives opposed giving the peacemakers this mission, however, on grounds that taking away arms would be taking away livelihoods and so must provoke a fight. Moreover, implementing Option 3 would mean five to ten years of nation-building. Other Committee members also favored the ball peen option.

At 0900 hours on 25 November, the President presided over a decisive meeting that Generals Powell and Hoar attended. The Chairman, who had consulted beforehand with Admiral Jeremiah and the Service Chiefs, advocated Option 3; so did USCINCCENT. Both officers felt that the situation had deteriorated to the point where, if the administration was determined to take an active role, large-scale intervention would be the best option. Secretary of Defense Cheney agreed with their assessment. But, Powell warned, it would be foolish not to anticipate taking on the full spectrum of Somalia's problems. If the United States intervened, other consequences would follow and getting out would prove difficult.

President Bush selected Option 3—the sledge-hammer. That, conferees noted, meant trying to restore a stable security environment for delivering humanitarian aid and could lead to confronting the warlords and disarming the factions. Powell urged that Ambassador Robert Oakley be called out of retirement and appointed special envoy. He had been Ambassador to Somalia in 1983-84 and, during 1987-88, had worked under Powell on the NSC Staff as Director for Middle East and South Asian affairs. The Chairman saw Oakley as a man who could harmonize Defense's concerns with the incoming administration's objectives.[12] Later that day, Acting Secretary of State Eagleburger informed Boutros-Ghali that, if the Security Council authorized member states to use force in order to ensure the delivery of relief supplies, the United States stood ready to take the lead in organizing and commanding such an operation.

Some Joint Staff officers thought that General Powell and Admiral Jeremiah had changed position because they recognized that President Bush wanted to use Option 3, not the "ball peen" approach. That was not so. General Powell accepted the necessity of intervention reluctantly, and rated Option 3 as the only realistic course of action if something had to be done. Both he and Jeremiah felt that, even though the UN had not made the right commitment, action was necessary. When Admiral Jeremiah told the Deputies Committee that "if you think U.S. forces are needed" on the ground "we can do the job," the Vice Chairman was neither advocating nor arguing against that course of action. Rather, he felt frustrated by the long-running discussion about military capabilities when, as he saw it, the issue was what policy should be adopted.[13]

Public sentiment obviously shaped President Bush's decision. The tragedy in Somalia was massive and television made it vivid. Preserving the UN's credibility, a concern that would loom large by mid-1993, was a secondary factor at this point. Only the United States possessed the capacity to act promptly. The Joint Staff, like the USCENTCOM staff, favored simply providing more air and sealift for the time being. In the Joint Staff's judgment, the difficulties attendant upon restoring order, bringing warlords to heel, and creating some semblance of a national polity accentuated the need for caution. The Chairman's Assistant, LTG Barry R. McCaffrey, USA, shared their view that nothing in Somalia involved any US national interest.[14] But General Powell, instead, chose immediate and large-scale intervention. The airlift was apparently helping the hinterlands, but it was very expensive and doing little for Mogadishu. If many thousands of lives were to be saved, a prompt commitment of US ground troops appeared necessary for opening ports and running convoys. The Chairman believed, as in the Persian Gulf, that intervention ought to be decisive. That was his consistent approach to the use of military power.

Defining a Mission

The President wanted US troops to enter Somalia as soon as possible and then be replaced by UN peacekeepers in the shortest feasible time. At the 25 November meeting, National Security Adviser Brent Scowcroft said that US troops must be out of Somalia by 20 January, when President Bush would leave office. General Powell and Secretary Cheney promptly advised Scowcroft that this deadline could not be met. Meantime, implementation of the decision to intervene was proceeding. If preparatory actions began at once, troops could land on 7 December. The carrier USS *Ranger* could arrive off Mogadishu on 1 December. One amphibious assault ship, USS *Tripoli*, would follow on 6 December; another, USS *Guam*, would be at Kuwait on 10 December. There was agreement within the administration that, for command arrangements, the Korean War precedent (i.e., a US commander carrying out Security Council resolutions) was the one to follow.[15]

Secretary General Boutros-Ghali informed the Security Council, on 29 November, that he saw five options:

1. Continue efforts to deploy forty-two hundred personnel for United Nations Operations in Somalia.

2. Withdraw all military forces.

3. Have UNOSOM stage a show of force followed, if necessary, by actual use of force in Mogadishu.

4. Have UN members, with the Security Council's authorization, conduct a country-wide operation that would create the conditions necessary to ensure the delivery of relief supplies.

5. Conduct a country-wide operation under UN command and control.

Boutros-Ghali rated options 1, 2 and 3 unacceptable. The UN, already overstretched by peacekeeping tasks, could not exercise command and control over an operation of the size and urgency required by option 5. That, he acknowledged, left no alternative to option 4.

On 1 December, the State Department sent Ambassador Perkins a draft Security Council resolution that would authorize UN members to use "all necessary means" in establishing a secure environment for relief operations. General Powell, at the same time, sent USCINCCENT a warning order:

When directed by the (National Command Authorities), US-CINCCENT will conduct military operations in Somalia to secure the major food distribution points and air/sea ports, guard relief convoys and relief organization operations, and assist relief organizations in providing humanitarian relief in Somalia under UN auspices."

Simultaneously, an NSC working group decided that selected US Defense attachés should be directed to solicit troop contributions for UN peacekeeping operations. Within the Joint Staff, J-3 began preparing a timeline for the first, peace-enforcing phase of operations; the J-4 addressed what air and sealift the United States should furnish, and J-5 set about defining the US role during subsequent peacekeeping operations.[16]

Secretary General Boutros-Ghali wanted to delete two paragraphs from the State Department's draft UN resolution. The first of these paragraphs urged expeditious deployment of thirty-five hundred more UNOSOM peacekeepers. The second stated that UNOSOM would keep functioning while a US-led coalition intervened, and that UNOSOM's commander would serve as deputy to the US commander. General Powell opposed making these deletions. In his judgment, separating UNOSOM from the US-led coalition could make the coalition appear too much like a US undertaking and thus delay the transition to UNOSOM. Powell believed that UNOSOM's mandate—unlike that of the US-led coalition—should be very broad and include political reconciliation among Somalis, restoration of security, humanitarian relief, nation-building, and creation of a police force. He would let the US commander decide which Somalis should be disarmed and did not want, during this opening phase, to distinguish the peacemakers from the peacekeepers.[17]

Nonetheless, the US draft was amended largely as Boutros-Ghali wished. Resolution 794, approved by the Security Council on 3 December, authorized the Secretary General and member states to "use all necessary means to establish as soon as possible a secure environment for humanitarian relief operations in Somalia." All members "in a position to do so" were asked to provide troops or contributions, the latter either in cash or in kind. Deployment of thirty–five hundred more UNOSOM troops was to proceed at the Secretary General's direction, based upon how he assessed conditions on the ground. The paragraph about UNOSOM's commander becoming deputy to a US officer disappeared.[18]

President Bush, on 4 December, publicly announced that US ground troops would enter Somalia in what was now christened Operation RESTORE HOPE. As General Powell had urged, Bush appointed Ambassador Robert Oakley to be his Special Envoy to Somalia. That same day, through a letter to Boutros-Ghali, the President emphasized that the US-led peacemaking or peace-enforcing coalition should have a limited, specific mission: Creating conditions that would allow starving Somalis to be fed and make possible the later transfer of this security function to a UN peacekeeping force. By 7 December, twelve countries had offered 13,650 troops for the US-led coalition; fourteen more nations were considering manpower contributions. Moreover, five countries had offered 5,653 personnel for UNOSOM's peacekeeping duties and another twenty were weighing participation.[19]

Back on 2 December, General Powell had sent General Hoar a planning order that assigned USCENTCOM an added mission: "disarm, as necessary, forces which interfere with humanitarian relief operations." An "execute" order contained that same language. On 6 December, after Hoar protested directly to the Chairman, an amendment deleted that added mission. Then USCINCCENT's mission was to secure air and seaports, ground routes and major relief centers; provide a secure environment, and protect and assist UN and non-government humanitarian and relief organizations. But Boutros-Ghali saw matters differently. Any forceful action, he told President Bush on 8 December, must ensure that at least the factions' heavy weapons were neutralized. Boutros-Ghali deemed it essential that the purpose of intervention should be to "create a secure environment throughout Somalia and that this should be apparent from the outset."[20] The Bush administration, however, limited neutralization to weaponry that could interfere with relief work. It also refused to deploy any US troops into northern Somalia because no humanitarian need existed there. The only reason for going north would be to deal with the entirely different problem of a breakaway "Somaliland" regime.

Coalition Forces Enter Somalia

Operation RESTORE HOPE, meanwhile, moved forward at a rapid pace. The 1st Marine Division at Camp Pendleton, California, was slated to be the major US element. On 26 November, Brigadier Generals David C. Meade and Richard A. Chilcoat, USA, came to J-3 JOD and recommended that the 101st Airborne Division (Air Assault) take part also. This division was well suited to covering wide areas. The drawback lay in its deployment requirements; much more air and sealift was needed to move helicopters and keep them fuelled than would be required for a light division. Soon afterward, the Army decided to use the 10th Mountain Division instead. Prior to this time, J-3 had been looking for units that could be deployed to protect the five hundred Pakistanis at Mogadishu airport. The Army as well as the Marine Corps had identified such units, and the 10th Mountain Division had not been mentioned.[21]

On 3 December, General Hoar asked for more forces. The main addition consisted of the most of the 10th Mountain Division. Hoar's other requests included: from the Army, combat support, combat service support and aviation units; from Special Operations Command, one active-duty psychological warfare operations battalion as well as civil affairs units from the Reserve Component; from the Air Force, one tactical airlift squadron (-); and from the Navy, one construction regiment (-). On 5 December, the Chairman told USCINCCENT that the National Command Authority had ordered execution of Operation RESTORE HOPE. Hoar was given virtually all the additional forces he had requested. Two brigades from the 10th Mountain Division did deploy, but enough contributions came from other countries to make dispatch of the whole division unnecessary.[22] The major US units assigned to RESTORE HOPE were: 1st Marine Expeditionary Force from Camp Pendleton, California, 16,800 personnel; 10th Mountain Division (-) from Fort Drum, New York, 10,200 personnel; and the offshore Marine Expeditionary Unit, 1,800 personnel.

The Joint Staff worked with the State Department to identify and obtain host nation approval for aircraft staging and refueling at Lajes in the Azores, Torrejon and Moron in Spain, Sigonella in Sicily, Cairo, Djibouti, Addis Ababa, Mombasa in Kenya, and Oman. Some personnel went to Aden, but they were withdrawn after a bomb exploded in their hotel. As soon as troop movements began, the focus of operations moved to the US Transportation Command (USTRANS-COM) and USCENTCOM. By 6 December, twelve KC-135A tankers had deployed to Lajes and twelve more to Moron; two Fast Sealift Ships were moving to Bayonne, New Jersey, and Wilmington, Delaware; the Military Traffic Management Command was organizing rail movements between the 10th Mountain Division's base at Fort Drum, New York, and Bayonne.[23]

During the pre-dawn hours of 9 December, Marines and Navy SEALs landed at Mogadishu. They came ashore unopposed but surrounded by journalists and camera crews. A small French Foreign Legion contingent from Djibouti joined the Marines. Lieutenant General Robert B. Johnston, Commanding General, I

Marine Expeditionary Force (MEF), arrived in Mogadishu on 10 December and became the Commander, Joint Task Force (JTF), Somalia.

Before RESTORE HOPE began, USCENTCOM had prepared a concept of operations with four slow-paced phases:

Phase I, D-Day (9 December) through D+24: Embarked Marines would secure the port and airfield at Mogadishu. Follow-on Marines from California and initial Army elements would occupy Baidoa and Baledogle, which had an airfield about seventy miles northwest of Mogadishu.

Phase II, D+24 through D+90: An Army brigade would secure the lodgement area around Baidoa. Relief centers at Belet Uen, Oddur and Gialalassi would be occupied.

Phase III, D+90 through D+180: The port and airfield at Kismayo, the land route between Baidoa and Bardera, and Bardera itself would be secured.

Phase IV, D+180 through D+240: Responsibility would be transferred to a UN peacekeeping force.

Instead, largely because Somali warlords did not resist, US and coalition peacemakers attained their objectives far ahead of schedule. Phase I was completed on D+7, 16 December, when Marines entered Baidoa. By then, 2,800 Marines and 170 Army troops were on the ground in Somalia. Because Marines secured Baledogle airfield so promptly, the 2d Brigade, 10th Mountain Division deployed to Baledogle and then to Kismayo, instead of Baidoa as originally planned. Army and Marine units arrived at Kismayo on D+11, 20 December; Marines reached Bardera on D+15, 24 December.[24]

The air and sealift had been set in motion at the beginning of December. Five ships from the Maritime Prepositioning Force were deployed, four from Diego Garcia in the Indian Ocean and one from the Marianas. By 15 December, five Fast Sealift Ships needed to carry the 10th Mountain Division's equipment had been activated. USTRANSCOM reported that the Army's lack of validated movement requirements in the Joint Operational Planning and Execution System (JOPES) had forced USTRANSCOM into an ad hoc "push" system based upon telephone and message traffic. Aircraft, as a result, were flying with inefficient loads.[25] The 10th Mountain Division's main deployment took place between 23 December and 6 January; the movement was not flawless. The Army loaded ships with equipment that had not been listed in the Time-Phased Force Deployment Data (TPFDD). Moreover, the Army's pre-positioned equipment afloat could not be offloaded for RESTORE HOPE. Shallow harbors in Somalia, lack of cranes in the port, and the reluctance of civilian captains to enter potentially hazardous waters stalled offloading and created a queue outside Mogadishu so long that the Army ships eventually left.

Setting Limits on the US Role

In Mogadishu, Baidoa, and Kismayo, the arrival of US and coalition forces quickly ended the worst disorders and allowed food distribution to resume. Even before Marines landed, the administration had promulgated guidance that would tightly limit the US-led coalition's role in disarming factions. On 8 December, a message cleared by the Chairman, OSD and the NSC transmitted Acting Secretary of State Eagleburger's instructions to Lieutenant General Johnston to make the following points during his first meeting with Somali warlords: No weapons at all would be permitted in "exclusion areas," which at the outset would include Mogadishu's port and airfield, the US Embassy compound (where the Joint Task Force would establish its headquarters), as well as the areas immediately around them. Within the JTF area of operations, heavy weapons would be permitted only in "cantonment areas," meaning those small and clearly defined areas where personnel and equipment would be encamped.[26]

On 9 December, Rear Admiral Bowman and Ambassador Brandon Grove met with Under Secretary Goulding and Assistant Secretary General Kofi Annan. The UN officials believed that calling the US-led coalition a "unified command" was misleading. They preferred "Unified Task Force for Somalia." Soon afterward, the administration accepted "UNITAF" as the term to be used. Goulding and Annan also argued strongly that now was the best time to disarm as many Somalis as possible throughout the country and pressed hard for deploying UNITAF into northern Somalia. Bowman and Grove said that some elements might go north, but only if they were transferred to the control of the United Nations Operations in Somalia (UNOSOM).[27]

Next day, in Washington, the NSC Core Group agreed that UNOSOM II would need a stronger mandate than Security Council Resolution 775 had given the original UNOSOM.[28] The State Department was directed to prepare a draft resolution. The Joint Staff was instructed to prepare a paper describing what UNOSOM II ought to look like, and what units might participate in it. Already, the Joint Staff was working to bring advance elements from Jordan, Kuwait, Morocco, Nigeria, Turkey, Saudi Arabia and the United Arab Emirates into Mogadishu as soon as possible. On 11 December, the NSC Deputies Committee decided that Secretary General Boutros-Ghali should be pressed even harder to endorse a larger UNOSOM II and a stronger Security Council mandate.[29]

The J-5 MEAF looked at whether and how the United States should participate in UNOSOM II. There seemed to be only two possibilities. First, withdraw US forces completely once a secure environment had been established. That course of action risked a subsequent deterioration and a possible collapse of the whole humanitarian and reconstruction effort. Second, contribute unique US capabilities—communications, engineers, logistic support, air traffic control, medical care, civil affairs—to UNOSOM II. General Powell strongly and repeatedly pressed this point. The J-5 noted that UN peacekeeping operations in Cambodia required twelve infantry and seven engineer battalions. With still other UN operations pending, J-5 MEAF believed that few if any nations could spare medics and engineers for Somalia.[30]

Concurrently, the J-5 MEAF proposed that a new Security Council mandate for UNOSOM II should specify the following: an increase in size from 4,200 to 12-15,000 personnel; weaponry that was adequate to meet hostile challenges; rules of engagement permitting greater latitude for preventive actions, even the destruction of heavy weapons, and authority to help establish a Somali police force, which would be a critical early step toward national reconciliation and the full restoration of Somali sovereignty.

One crucial question—who would disarm the Somali factions—had gone unanswered. During a press conference on 14 December, General Hoar described disarmament as "a political issue, one that needs to be settled first and foremost by the Somalis." But, on that same day, Secretary General Boutros-Ghali stated that gaining control over the factions' arsenals was a "pre-requisite" to stability. In private meetings with US officials, Boutros-Ghali stressed his belief that UNITAF should disarm all factions. The J-5 MEAF, on 16 December, suggested a solution that would minimize UNITAF's task and facilitate a quick transition to UNOSOM II. After the Security Council approved a new mandate, the United States would urge UNITAF contributors to join UNOSOM II. Next, UNOSOM II would enter northern Somalia. With few exceptions, UNITAF and UNOSOM II would neutralize heavy and crew-served weapons wherever they were found. Then, as UNOSOM II in the north developed greater confidence and operational integrity while UNITAF continued pacifying southern and central Somalia, some UNITAF units could shift into UNOSOM II.[31]

By 20 December, more than thirty countries had pledged contributions, outstripping USCENTCOM's ability to provide new arrivals with command and, control and logistic support. For UNITAF, General Hoar had accepted more than ten thousand personnel from France, Belgium, Canada, the United Kingdom, India, Turkey, Egypt, Botswana, Morocco, Zimbabwe, Saudi Arabia and Kuwait. These nations were accepted on a priority basis because (1) it was deemed politically important to get Islamic, African and European forces on the ground quickly and (2) these countries had responded first and/or would provide their own transport and logistical support.[32] No contributor was refused; those offering the least self-sufficient forces simply were put at the end of the line. Some countries saw participation as a way to acquire equipment; a few used it to meet their payroll.

Secretary General Boutros-Ghali's report to the Security Council on 19 December did meet US desires by asking for an expanded military mandate for UNOSOM II, including substantially greater troop levels. He also argued for a slow area-by-area shift of control from UNITAF to UNOSOM II. But contrary to the US position, Boutros-Ghali recommended that UNITAF either disarm all organized factions and irregulars or at least confiscate their heavy weapons. Further, he proposed sending UNITAF forces into northern Somalia and postponing advanced planning for UNITAF's transition into UNOSOM II. Boutros-Ghali even wanted to define two conditions for UNITAF's withdrawal. First, heavy weapons belonging to the organized factions must be neutralized and brought under international control throughout Somalia. Second, heavy weapons belonging to "gangs" must be confiscated and destroyed throughout Somalia. The State Department, by contrast, had drafted a much less ambitious plan involving weapons-free security zones, voluntary surrender of heavy weapons, and involuntary disarming when weapons might directly impede humanitarian missions.[33]

The NSC Core Group, on 22 December, agreed that State and Defense would draft a message to Johnston and Ambassador Oakley authorizing the startup of a police force in Mogadishu. Also, State proposed (1) that UNOSOM troops—not US forces—be available for deployment to northern Somalia and (2) that the United States agree to such a mission once enough peacekeepers had arrived to replace US forces in the south. Next day, J-5 MEAF completed a study of how the transition from UNITAF to UNOSOM II could take place. Fully coordinated within the Joint Staff, cleared by USCENTCOM, and sent to other agencies for review, this study presented two options:

1. Lieutenant General Johnston would retain all peace enforcers under his control until UNITAF completed its mission. Concurrently, UNOSOM II would be activated as a separate but coordinated command, which would progressively assume control over sectors that UNITAF had made secure.

2. Lieutenant General Johnston would designate a section of his staff to control UNOSOM II peacekeepers. Headed by commander-designate of UNOSOM II, it would assume responsibility for sectors deemed secure and evolve into an independent staff.

In appraising these options, J-5 MEAF estimated that three to five thousand US personnel (e.g., supply, engineer and medical units) would be needed to support a UNOSOM II force of twelve to fifteen thousand. Moreover, even after the main body of US forces left Somalia, a small Quick Reaction Force (QRF) designed to respond to emergencies should be based offshore; it would gradually move back over the horizon.[34]

In Geneva, on 30 December, Under Secretary of State Wisner and Lieutenant General McCaffrey conferred with Boutros-Ghali. Wisner noted the time was right to pass a new Security Council resolution and move ahead with transferring responsibility to UNOSOM II. Boutros-Ghali replied that he preferred to wait until President-elect Clinton took office. After this meeting, the Secretary General went on to inspect UN relief operations in Sarajevo and then in Mogadishu. Boutros-Ghali ran a gamut of hostile demonstrators at both places. Lieutenant General Johnston told the Secretary General that Somali "technicals" had been taken into cantonments at Kismayo, Bardera and Baidoa; any technicals still active in Mogadishu would be eliminated. Johnston also said that he expected the security situation throughout Mogadishu to improve greatly by January's close. Nonetheless, Boutros-Ghali evidently felt unsettled enough to want clear directions from President Bush and President-elect Clinton before seeking a new Security Council mandate.[35]

On 6 January 1993, Rear Admiral Bowman attended what had become a weekly session at UN headquarters in New York. The Joint Staff regularly sent a small contingent of J-3, J-4, J-5 and J-6 officers to work with UN officials. These officers found no comparable staff expertise at UN headquarters—a weakness that would become more evident and more crippling as time went on. The UN head-quarters could barely support a US-led operation, much less a UN one.

Under Secretary General Goulding argued that northern Somalia be included in UNOSOM II planning. Bowman agreed to assist UN planning, provided that such plans did not interfere with UNITAF's withdrawal from the south. At General Powell's urging, the United States supported selecting a Turkish officer to command UNOSOM II. Goulding felt certain that the Secretary General would agree, but still wanted to look for a black African commander who presumably would be more congenial to Somalis.[36]

Meanwhile, the Bush administration had been soliciting contributions for UNOSOM II with good results. By early January offers of support totaled 31,200 personnel. Joint Staff officers reviewed these offers and helped draft the replies. About two-thirds of the potential contributors' forces would need logistic support; some proposed contingents would be coming with little more than their uniforms. Although the UN had the final word, a number of governments were discreetly discouraged or urged to postpone the arrival of their contingents. USCENTCOM hoped to bring in the more self-sufficient contributors first, in roughly the following order: Australia, Germany, India, Pakistan, Sweden, Jordan, New Zealand, United Arab Emirates, Nigeria, and Tunisia.[37]

Among all the potential contributors, Pakistan posed the most difficult problem for US policymakers. Since September, five hundred Pakistanis had been stationed around Mogadishu airport. Shortly after he decided upon US intervention, President Bush personally appealed to Pakistan's President for another, larger contribution. Generals Powell and Hoar pressed the matter because they saw this as an opportunity to restore close US-Pakistani ties. The Pakistanis offered a four thousand-man brigade. They wanted to deploy the brigade immediately as part of UNITAF and have it join UNOSOM II later. Hoar also wanted the Pakistanis to join UNITAF, thereby creating a solid foundation for the transition to UNOSOM II.

The Pakistanis wanted substantial amounts of US equipment to strengthen their brigade. But the 1985 Pressler Amendment to the Foreign Assistance Act of 1961 prohibited military assistance to Pakistan, unless the President certified that Pakistan did not possess a nuclear explosive device and that US assistance would reduce significantly the risk of Pakistan's acquiring one. The State Department and the NSC Staff felt that these restrictions, coupled with the Pakistanis' need for extensive support, would complicate the brigade's assignment to UNITAF. From the start, the Pakistani unit should be the anchor of UNOSOM II that would avoid Pressler

Amendment restrictions. From Islamabad, however, the US Ambassador warned that Pakistanis would resent a proposal to shift their contribution to UNOSOM II.

In mid-December 1992, the State Department drafted an interim reply that any US equipment should be supplied directly to the UN for use in Somalia only, so that the Pressler Amendment would not come into play. The Director, Joint Staff, concurred but recommended one addition: because logistical facilities in Somalia were so restricted, scheduling of the brigade's arrival must be coordinated through USCENTCOM.[38]

Early in February 1993, the J-5 MEAF proposed seeking a Presidential waiver of the Pressler Amendment, similar to what had been done during the 1980s. Instead, the administration decided that transport services and non-munitions articles (mostly trucks and trailers) would be leased to the United Nations. The UN, in turn, would lease them to the Pakistanis, who could use the equipment only while they were in Somalia as part of either UNITAF or UNOSOM II. The US Government then sought, from the UN Somalia Trust Fund, $7.8 million in reimbursement. The Pakistani advance element arrived in Mogadishu on 12 April; the brigade's main body followed two weeks later.[39]

Meanwhile, at a national reconciliation conference in Addis Ababa on 4-15 January, Somali factional leaders agreed that all militias should camp outside major towns and disarm by 1 March. But, as US officials had maintained from the very start of RESTORE HOPE, there could be no restoration of law and order without a national police force. Back on 21 December, Ambassador Oakley had urged the immediate start-up of a temporary local auxiliary guard force, under UNOSOM, followed by re-creation of a national police force. The Director, Joint Staff, proposed organizing an auxiliary guard force if UNITAF would cover the $100,000 cost of US trainers. On 30 December, the Deputies Committee agreed in principle. Two days later, the State Department instructed Ambassador Oakley to discuss this concept with UN Special Envoy Kittani.[40]

Oakley did not consider this step sufficient. On 12 January, he warned the State Department that problems resulting from the absence of a police force were "rapidly reaching crisis proportions." Increasingly, he reported, UNITAF troops as well as Somali civilians were becoming the victims of street crimes. The administration, however, still held that creating a national police force was a UN responsibility. The Germans, who had advised the Somalis on police problems from 1965 until 1990, were reluctant to take the lead. Italians wanted to play a major role, but US officials worried that their colonial rule had left a legacy of bitterness.

On 3 February, Assistant Secretary General Annan agreed to provide $2.4 million for an interim auxiliary force totaling about five thousand personnel countrywide; the US Government would be sole-source contractor.[41]

The police issue was part of a wider and graver question: Was the United Nations capable of shouldering burdens that temporarily were being borne by the United States? "The painful reality at UNOSOM," a US official cabled from Mogadishu on 8 January, "is that there is very little leadership, considerable inertia and low morale." The Secretary General's office had not been assigning motivated, qualified personnel to the effort. Special Envoy Kittani, whom US officials did not regard very highly in any case, had fallen ill and wanted to go back to New York. On 12 January, Ambassador Oakley reported that UN political and relief structures outside Mogadishu lay "in a state of catastrophic weakness and disorganization." Without a strong UN presence in the field, he warned, efforts to rebuild Somalia would collapse when the troops departed.[42] The new administration, however, proved slow in recognizing that UN weaknesses across the board were endangering the whole enterprise.

Accomplishing the Transition

When President Clinton took office on 20 January, UNITAF consisted of 24,500 US and about 13,000 non-US troops. For UNOSOM II, offers totaled about eighteen thousand personnel. Around seven thousand non-US personnel for UNOSOM II were actually in Somalia. It was assumed that the United States would contribute service and support units totaling several thousand personnel.

On 28 January, Lieutenant General Johnston reported that the factions had been largely neutralized and major weapons systems "reduced." Humanitarian aid was flowing throughout UNITAF's area of operations; local markets and commerce had reappeared. Consequently, Johnston considered UNITAF's mission in southern Somalia complete and the time ripe for transition to UNOSOM II.[43]

The Defense Department badly wanted a quick transition for budgetary reasons. As a response to a humanitarian emergency and, therefore, not a part of the Department's budget, Operation RESTORE HOPE was funded from the Services' operations and maintenance budgets. The Navy initially expressed reluctance; the Joint Staff J-4 appealed to the OSD Comptroller and the Navy made its funds available. Over three months, it was calculated, RESTORE HOPE would cost $560 million. As one of his last acts, Secretary of Defense Dick Cheney had submitted what he called a zero-sum supplemental appropriations request, in which he proposed reprogramming $560 million to offset the money taken from the Services' accounts.[44] In April 1993, Secretary of Defense Les Aspin asked Congress to shift $750 million from the Services' procurement and research and development appropriations to their operations, maintenance and personnel accounts. This was done in July by Public Law 103-50. The cost of UNITAF came to $692.2 million, none of it reimbursable by the UN.[45]

The new administration promptly scheduled a Deputies Committee meeting to review and validate overall US strategy for Somalia. At this point, the Joint Staff represented the best repository of continuity, particularly in its understanding of the UN's weaknesses. Officers from the J-5 MEAF recommended creating a credible security and humanitarian role for the United Nations; that meant insuring the success of UNOSOM II. A new Security Council resolution should allow the utmost flexibility in carrying out peacekeeping operations.[46]

UNOSOM II could not function without sizeable US logistic support. Accordingly, US logistics units would be placed under UNOSOM II. However, a land-based quick reaction force made up of US troops would remain under USCENTCOM and the decision to employ US combat forces would stay in US hands.

As of late January, the timelines assumed for US military planning ran as follows:

March-April 1993: UNITAF transfers responsibilities to UNOSOM II.

May 1993: US forces in Somalia are reduced to about six thousand personnel.

Autumn 1993: The US quick reaction force withdraws from Somalia, and a Marine Amphibious Ready Group assumes its function.

December 1993: The US contribution to UNOSOM II totals around three thousand personnel.

December 1994: UNOSOM II withdraws, following the creation of a government of national unity.

The Joint Staff could not avoid purely political issues but sought to distance itself from them. Officers from J-5 MEAF argued that political reconciliation must be accomplished under UN rather than US leadership. By far the best course lay in former Special Envoy Sahnoun's "bottom up" approach, revitalizing the system of clan elders, mobilizing local community action groups, and re-creating a police force.[47]

The new Deputies Committee convened on 25 January. Samuel Berger, Deputy Assistant to the President for National Security Affairs, chaired the meeting. He learned that anti-American sentiment among Somalis was increasing. Awe of US troops was declining, and Somalis were testing them. Still, the level of violence was no higher than originally expected. It was made clear that President Clinton supported all his predecessor's policies except willingness to play a major part in UNOSOM II. During the transition, outgoing officials had said that the United States might contribute a quick reaction force and a few logistic units. Anything more would have to be discussed with the President. Admiral Jeremiah assured the Deputies that he felt comfortable about putting American troops in UNOSOM II under a foreign commander and wanted the foreign officer to take up his post as soon as possible.[48]

Frank Wisner, the Under Secretary of Defense for Policy-designate, outlined a proposed course of action. In a memorandum to Secretary of Defense Les Aspin, dated 27 January, he stated that no time limit could be placed upon US logistic support for UNOSOM II. President Clinton needed to know that such an extended commitment was the price of success. Also, the new Secretary of State should persuade Boutros-Ghali to do several things. First, support a Security Council resolution that contained language from Chapter VII dealing with "enforcement." According to Chapter VII, the Security Council could decide whether a threat to peace, breach of peace, or act of aggression had occurred and then authorize measures "to maintain or restore international peace and security." Second, name a UNOSOM II commander, preferably a Turk, who was acceptable to the United States. Third, increase and improve UN staff support. Fourth, start organizing a police force under UNITAF and then under UNOSOM II.[49]

Concurrently, General Hoar informed the Joint Staff that forces adequate to accomplish UNITAF's mission were either in Somalia or programmed to arrive there. Therefore, any additional offers should be directed to the UN and UNOSOM II. Hoar also sent Chairman Powell a proposed plan for withdrawing US forces:

Phase I: Reduce to 15,500 troops ashore and 4,500 afloat, with the Army and Marine Corps being cut to one reinforced brigade each.

Phase II: Reduce to twelve thousand troops ashore and four thousand afloat, leaving the Army and the Marine Corps with one under-strength brigade each. UNITAF's area of operations had been split into nine humanitarian relief sectors. Now, sector-by-sector, UNITAF should start handing over responsibility to UNOSOM II.

Phase III: Reduce to six thousand troops ashore and four thousand afloat, leaving in Somalia only a quick reaction force and limited logistic support units.

Phase IV: Reduce to fourteen hundred troops ashore and four thousand afloat, moving the quick reaction force to ships that were over the horizon and leaving logistic support units ashore.[50]

The NSC Principals Committee, including General Powell, met on 28 January and recommended initially committing as many as four thousand support and logistic troops to UNOSOM II. But, as new civilian officials evidently were not aware, the UN's ability to take on major tasks still was very much in question. For example, US initiatives had laid the groundwork for starting up an interim auxiliary police force. On 31 January, however, Lieutenant General Johnston voiced doubts that UN officials were truly committed to establishing it. Ambassador Oakley also warned that an "underlying culture of passivity and the bureaucratic manner in which all UNOSOM activities are conducted" boded ill for the future.[51]

President Clinton ordered an interdepartmental review of US policy. According to his directive, the review would focus upon what could be done to prevent Somalia from sliding back into anarchy and famine. The State and Defense Departments would develop a plan for recruiting, deploying, and equipping an adequate force for UNOSOM II. The Joint Chiefs of Staff were told to examine issues involving the Quick Reaction Force: the criteria for its withdrawal; the size and speed of any return; its availability for use in northern Somalia; and its command relationship with UNOSOM II.[52]

Late in February, an interagency working group chaired by Assistant Secretary of State Cohen reviewed the responses to the President's directive. According to the National Intelligence Council, creation of a stable society could take years and require prolonged outside intervention and guidance. The interagency group agreed that, while the prospects for a new Somali political order appeared limited at best, a "bottom up" approach emphasizing local and regional governments had the best chance of succeeding. The Security Council still needed to give UNOSOM II a broader mandate; energetic US and international contributions to bolster the UN staff were vital. The UN enjoyed little credit with Somalis; they, as well as prospective donors to UNOSOM II, saw a strong US presence as critical.

Nonetheless, from now on, other donors must provide the bulk of aid; US assistance should serve only as a catalyst.[53]

By early March, the troop list of major contributors to UNITAF peacemaking and then to UNOSOM II peacekeeping read as follows:

Forces Projected

Donor Nation	UNITAF Forces	For UNOSOM II
Australia	1129	45
Belgium	859	875
Canada	1039	0
France	1572	1000
Germany	55	1500 (uncertain)
India	189	4000 (uncertain)
Indonesia	0	850
Italy	3183	2500
Jordan	0	900
Morocco	1264	1250 (uncertain)
Pakistan	880	4000
Saudi Arabia	669	669
Turkey	300	300
United States	13,884	4000

The Germans, Indians and Moroccans eventually would come, but the Indonesians and Jordanians would not.

Secretary General Boutros-Ghali selected Lieutenant General Cevik Bir of Turkey to command UNOSOM II; Bir took command on 8 March. On 26 March, the UN Security Council approved Resolution 814, the long-sought mandate based upon Chapter VII of the UN Charter. It authorized an expanded UNOSOM

II to operate until 31 October 1993, emphasized the "crucial importance of disarmament" and demanded that all Somali parties comply fully with the commitments made at Addis Ababa. The UNOSOM II Force Commander would "assume responsibility for the consolidation, expansion, and maintenance of a secure environment throughout Somalia," as well as organizing "a prompt, smooth and phased transition from UNITAF to UNOSOM II." Resolution 814 had been drafted by US government agencies, but the administration did not appreciate how difficult achieving those objectives would prove and how deeply the United States would have to involve itself in that effort.

A Mixed Appraisal

Was the glass of reconstruction and reconciliation half full or half empty? Starvation had practically ceased but organized thievery was increasing and basic services like water and electricity still had not been restored in most cities and towns. No significant steps had been taken toward a national police force, but auxiliary police forces now totaled over five thousand. On 29 March, meeting again at Addis Ababa, representatives from fifteen Somali factions agreed that a transitional national council would act as the country's principal political authority. The council would work with relief agencies and with UNOSOM II to carry out humanitarian assistance programs as well as cease-fire and disarmament accords. However, disarmament agreements had not been widely carried out, and none of the warlords showed willingness to compromise or negotiate in good faith.

Concurrently, the administration took several steps to bolster the UN's venture in peacekeeping. Admiral Howe succeeded Ismet Kittani as the Secretary General's Special Representative.[54] Several US military and Foreign Service personnel also took up posts in Mogadishu, where they bolstered UN officials. Colonel Wahlquist became military advisor to the US Liaison Office in Mogadishu, where he worked under Ambassador Robert Gosende. Ambassador Oakley had returned home early in March.

The transition did proceed promptly and smoothly. On 29 March, the Deputies Committee agreed that the US contribution to UNOSOM II should stay at four thousand logistics and Quick Reaction Force troops through August 1993, then decrease to fourteen hundred by January 1994.[55] Major General Thomas M. Montgomery, USA, had arrived to take up the posts of Commander, US Forces Somalia, and Deputy Force Commander of UNOSOM II. On 5 April, General Powell went to Mogadishu where Bir and Montgomery told him that they were ready to make a transfer by the end of May. Lieutenant General Bir withheld his final consent, though, until late in April when Lieutenant General Johnston submitted a "worst case scenario" for Mogadishu. This scenario projected street riots like those of late February, which Bir felt UNOSOM II would be able to handle. The final act took place on 4 May, earlier than originally planned, when Johnston dissolved UNITAF and turned over all its responsibilities to UNOSOM II and its Force Commander, Lieutenant General Cevik Bir.

Central Command had expected the quick reaction force to consist, from the start, of a Marine Expeditionary Unit (MEU) stationed offshore. The French, however, warned General Hoar that they would withdraw unless some US ground combat forces stayed in Somalia. Consequently, Hoar created a force ashore whose organization and equipment resembled that of a MEU. He assigned it no armor for several reasons. Things were quiet and the force was supposed to serve a political purpose. Also, USCENTCOM saw no reason to deploy a heavy force on land that soon would transition to a light one offshore. The rabbit warrens of Mogadishu were judged to not be good places to commit armor, and lighter units could be moved to the interior more rapidly by airlift.[56]

Through PDD/NSC-6, dated 19 May, President Clinton charted a course for the longer term. He approved Chairman Powell's recommendation that two groups of US forces participate in UNOSOM II. First, the support troops—as many as four thousand in May but dropping to fourteen hundred by January 1994—would be under the UN's operational control and work for Lieutenant General Bir. Second, the Quick Reaction Force would stay under USCINCCENT's command and operational control. The US and the UN would specify emergency situations for employing the QRF. When it deployed in the field, the QRF would work for the Commander of UNOSOM II and serve under the tactical control of Major General Montgomery. In some circumstances, the QRF might take tactical direction from the UNOSOM sector commander. Plans should be made to withdraw the QRF from Somalia during the summer of 1993, but redeployment would occur only upon the President's order.

President Clinton also directed a range of efforts in the security, humanitarian and political areas. These included:

1. Supporting a program to collect heavy weapons and, in the case of renewed fighting, using enforcement power; helping to create a professional police force, at the regional as well as national level, as soon as possible; and considering providing Special Operations Forces if required.

2. Pressing other donors to make good their aid pledges for humanitarian relief and reconstruction.

3. Ensuring that UNOSOM II remained actively involved in nation-building, and in supporting the establishment of structures restoring essential public services based upon legitimately vested authorities.

Periodically, the Deputies Committee would review progress—including the issue of major force withdrawals—until all US forces left Somalia.[57]

Just after President Clinton took office, Ambassador Oakley had submitted an optimistic appraisal: "The problems of Somalia are solvable. Investments of time, resources, and forces are needed to make it work. UNITAF's role to 'jump start' the process and create the immediate security environment has been accomplished." With hindsight, however, Admiral Jeremiah felt that critical time was lost during the Clinton administration's break-in period. New officials overrated the UN's capabilities. In Jeremiah's view, the White House kept operating for some time in a campaign mode, skeptical about the views of officials carried over from the Bush administration and of those who had not been on the election team. Partly as a result, he believed, the US government never committed enough resources to UNOSOM II. Already, for example, it was clear that creation of a police force depended entirely upon US efforts.[58]

Operation RESTORE HOPE certainly could be rated a success from the standpoint of humanitarian relief. By the spring of 1993, only small pockets of Somalis still needed help to avert starvation. Mogadishu was quiet, and gangs no longer roamed the countryside. From the outset, General Powell, Admiral Jeremiah and the Joint Staff had worked to keep the US-led intervention brief and a quick turnover from UNITAF to UNOSOM II was accomplished. But the UN remained extremely dependent upon US logistical support, to the point that logistic deficiencies influenced acceptance of troop offers. Few nations were capable of providing for their own essential needs; US troops had to provide most of them with direct support, a mission not foreseen in earlier planning. If the experience of RESTORE HOPE is a guide, US logistic troops will be among the first in and last out during most such UN operations.

A much graver difficulty flowed from the decision to put tight limits upon UNITAF's disarmament efforts. After things went awry during the summer and autumn of 1993, critics would claim that a great opportunity had been missed back in December. Warlords then were so overawed by US power, they said, that the factions in Mogadishu could have been completely disarmed. Some civilians on the NSC Staff would have preferred to do more disarming but the White House deferred to the military commander on the scene, whose judgment was backed by Admiral Jeremiah and General Powell. Lieutenant General Johnston worried that house-to-house disarming—as opposed to confiscating only heavy weapons and "technicals"—might keep UNITAF operating indefinitely. In practical terms, these officers felt certain, disarming an entire city was an impossible task. Could even a single street in a large American city be kept completely disarmed? Moreover, a humanitarian mission would have changed into a politico-military operation. Weapons seizures, consequently, did not go beyond what was necessary to insure that relief convoys moved safely. Late in February, despite the presence of US and Belgian troops in Kismayo, fighters led by Siad Barre's son-in-law attacked Aideed's allies and drove them out of the city. In April, the Canadian brigade declared Belet Uen pacified after forcing militiamen to withdraw rather than disarming them. UNITAF tried to intimidate the warlords but not overtly interfere with them; Ambassador Oakley used the analogy of plucking a chicken feather by feather. But ultimately there was no way to keep the mission purely humanitarian. The effort at political reconstruction threatened certain warlords' power and soon led to a confrontation with UNOSOM. Ali Mahdi, for example, put all his technicals in a cantonment by mid-February. Aideed, by contrast, quietly moved his technicals as well as much other equipment out of Mogadishu.

The US government had to decide how much to do in Somalia and how much it should leave to the UN. Growing doubts about the UN's ability to carry out the tasks of security, reconciliation and reconstruction never led any US officers or civilian officials to recommend delaying the turnover. Ambassador Oakley promptly identified re-creating the national police force as a vital task, for example, yet only the most modest steps were started. The new administration's undue optimism about UN capabilities only widened the gap between expectation and reality. In May 1993, when Force Command headquarters was staffed at only twenty-two percent of its authorized strength, UNOSOM II shouldered a much heavier burden than it was ready to bear.

Chapter 3
"Necessary Measures"

Early in June, one month after it had assumed UNITAF's responsibilities, UNOSOM II contained about eighteen thousand personnel from nineteen countries; Belgium, France, Italy, Morocco, Pakistan and the United States were its main contributors. An Indian brigade, expected in April, did not arrive until September. The Australians and Canadians, two of the best-equipped contingents, departed in mid-May and early June.

UNOSOM II barely had begun functioning before strains among its members and friction between the peace enforcers and Somali factions began eroding UNOSOM's ability to carry out its mandate. Pakistanis, who formed the largest contingent, wanted to reach out to their fellow-Muslims. The Pakistanis really were expected to be a presence rather than a fighting force. Major General Montgomery was well aware of the dangerous environment—his own vehicle had been hit by bullets in April—but did not anticipate the scale of violence that erupted.

Mohammed Farah Aideed evidently worried that the "bottom up" strategy would undercut his power. UNOSOM headquarters, collaborating with the Pakistani contingent, prepared a plan to conduct inventories at five Authorized Weapon Storage Sites in Mogadishu that Aideed's Somali National Alliance (SNA) militia was allowed to maintain. The plan was approved by Major General Montgomery and by Jonathan Howe.[1] Five teams, each accompanied by one Pakistani company, carried out the inspections on 5 June. The SNA had been notified by UNOSOM the night before. "Radio Aideed" was collocated with one site, and Aideed apparently feared that there might be a raid on the transmitter as well. After the inspections were completed, a Pakistani convoy drove into what UNOSOM headquarters later called "a carefully prepared three-sided ambush" laid by Aideed's militiamen; twenty-four Pakistanis were killed. Simultaneous incidents, obviously coordinated, occurred elsewhere in Mogadishu.

Resolution 837

The UN and the US government acted swiftly to show their anger and resolve. Generals Powell and Hoar had rated the Pakistani contribution as crucial to

UNOSOM's success. US civilian officials believed that the coalition could not be sustained unless a hard stand was taken. Since Aideed had agreed to UNITAF's entry and to the Addis Ababa accord on nation-building, there was strong feeling among US, UN and Pakistani officials that he had betrayed those commitments and acted as a rogue. Pakistan's representative on the Security Council became the prime mover in pushing for prompt action. On Saturday, 5 June, Joint Staff officers discussed what sanctions the Security Council could apply to a situation where, since there was no central government, the laws of armed conflict did not apply. A draft resolution sent from New York specified Aideed by name as the target of UN reaction. Rear Admiral Bowman and Lieutenant General McCaffrey took charge of Joint Staff efforts on Sunday, 6 June. Officers from several directorates participated. Around 1100 hours, the NSC Staff sent them a proposed Security Council resolution. McCaffrey then held a telephone conference with representatives from other agencies. They discussed a number of options, including holding Aideed aboard an Egyptian ship and trying him in Pakistan. Late in the afternoon, a draft was forwarded to the US Delegation in New York. Approved by the Security Council that same evening, Resolution 837 authorized Secretary General Boutros-Ghali "to take all necessary measures" against those responsible for the attack as well as those who had incited it, including "the investigation of their actions and their arrest and detention for prosecution, trial and punishment." Neither General Powell nor Admiral Jeremiah recalled having seen the final version that went to New York; Lieutenant General McCaffrey had spoken frequently by telephone with both officers. The Chairman did ask National Security Adviser Anthony Lake that the resolution make no mention of Aideed, and this was done.[2]

Written in haste, Resolution 837 proved to be a turning point, a fact that no one appreciated at the time. A more deliberate review might have drawn attention to its potential pitfalls. After the turnover to UNOSOM on 4 May, no interagency body had met continuously to monitor the Somali situation. It had been assumed that UNOSOM II would face bandits, not centrally directed guerrillas. The Chairman's oral guidance to Major General Montgomery was neither to make UNOSOM II an American show nor allow it to fail. The United States wanted UNOSOM II to succeed without having the US military play a prominent role— and these goals would prove mutually exclusive.

On 6 June, General Hoar sent the Joint Staff a request for four AC-130 gunships. Next day, the Secretary General's Military Adviser gave the US Delegation three "notes verbales" asking for one company of tanks with US crews, sixty M-113

APCs to be driven by UNOSOM personnel, and four attack helicopters. On 8 June, Special Representative Howe asked that the United States station an amphibious ready group and perhaps an aircraft carrier offshore and deploy the following reinforcements: six attack and four CH-47 cargo helicopters, OH-58D observation helicopters or an equivalent; AC-130 gunships; two C-130s; one tank company and at least sixteen APCs; A-10 attack aircraft or a similar capability; riot control equipment; Special Operations Forces; and sea logistics.[3] Both Lieutenant General Bir and Major General Montgomery supported what Joint Staff officers dubbed Jonathan Howe's "wish list." Howe contemplated deploying only six or at most twenty SOF personnel; this was the first of his many requests for SOF.

The administration decided to position an ARG offshore and send AC-130s, eight attack and two observation helicopters, sixty M-113s, lift for Turkish tanks, and riot control equipment. It did not provide an aircraft carrier, A-10s, sea logistics, a US tank company, or Special Operations Forces. By 8 June, before most of this equipment had arrived but with US urging, UNOSOM headquarters worked out a plan to attack Aideed's weapons storage sites and his stronghold near UN headquarters. Four AC-130s, flying from Djibouti and working in tandem with US Army Cobra gunships, would provide the backbone for this operation.[4]

Moroccan and Pakistani troops, on 7 June, conducted clearing operations along 21 October Road, which was the UNOSOM forces' main supply route. On 11 June, Secretary of State Warren Christopher informed the US Delegation to the United Nations that Aideed and the SNA "should no longer be allowed to participate in the UN peace process in Somalia." Aideed's Habir Gidr sub-clan should remain involved but not under his leadership. Next day, UNOSOM troops raided SNA enclaves and disabled "Radio Aideed."[5]

During 13-14 June, AC-130 gunships carried out strikes to destroy arms caches. Generals Powell and Hoar received detailed briefings about the plan for UNOSOM's next offensive against Aideed's strongholds. After nighttime attacks by AC-130s, troops would surround the area, confiscate weapons and detain militiamen. SOF would carry out command, control and communications functions, with the QRF remaining in reserve. Both Howe and Boutros-Ghali were pressing, without success, for deployment of SOF troops who would track and capture Aideed and his lieutenants. On 16 June an obviously disturbed Secretary of State Warren Christopher asked Chairman Powell whether another search and arrest mission would take place in the near future. The answers that had been given thus far, according to Christopher, were "yes" and "maybe yes." Major

General Montgomery, the Secretary related, believed that the operation had to be carried out promptly if it was to be done at all. French, Italian, Moroccan and Pakistani ground troops were slated for use, with a US QRF providing air cover and a ground reserve. But the French and probably Moroccan troops would be leaving Mogadishu and returning to Baidoa within twenty-four hours. Consequently, Christopher was concerned that Aideed could regain the initiative unless UNOSOM acted. The operation did take place on 17 June, and much materiel was seized. But, much more significantly, this proved to be UNOSOM's last major offensive effort. Pakistanis and Moroccans (the latter lost five dead and thirty-nine wounded on 17 June) would not continue offensive operations, and the French, under orders from Paris, redeployed to Baidoa.[6]

Aideed Becomes the "Center of Gravity"

Meanwhile, through a paper prepared for use at a Deputies Committee meeting, officers in J-5 MEAF had raised a broader issue: "The military is supplying the brawn, but who, if anyone, is supplying the brain? Is there a political road map to follow?" The mapmakers were not of one mind. On 21 June, the State Department circulated a draft message for Annan and Howe: Aideed's removal as a major factor in Somalia's political and military landscape—something that State treated as already having been accomplished—provided a "striking opportunity" to move forward with reconciliation and reconstruction. Simultaneously, however, a Defense Intelligence Report concluded that Aideed remained defiant, portraying himself as a victim of UN aggression, and that his faction still controlled that part of Mogadishu where the SNA had its strongholds.[7] In Mogadishu, on 2 July, Italian troops were ambushed near a pasta factory, losing three killed and twenty-one wounded.

Ground and air elements of the US QRF destroyed an SNA command and control center on 12 July, killing Habr Gidr elders. Until this time, people living in a targeted area had been given prior warning by airborne loudspeakers. Many UNOSOM partners, who had not been consulted beforehand, considered this attack too provocative and an escalation of violence. Worse, this attack affected Somali attitudes as much as the 5 June attack had influenced attitudes within UNOSOM. The SNA's attitude hardened, and it attracted support from other sub-clans. By mid-July, firefights between UNOSOM troops and Aideed's militia were occurring almost daily. US intelligence indicated that Aideed felt that he could bleed UNOSOM with small-scale attacks and ultimately face it down. If UNOSOM II continued on course, it risked becoming a hostage to banditry and feuding militias, just like the initial group of five hundred Pakistanis assigned to UNOSOM.

Already, the UN's credibility was sinking while Aideed was emerging as a folk hero. On 17 June, Jonathan Howe declared Aideed an outlaw for having incited the 5 June attack; a UN jurist reviewed the evidence and concluded that there were grounds for arrest. Howe moved carefully on this matter, consulting a number of times with Kofi Annan and then talking with Boutros-Ghali. Major General Montgomery favored seizing Aideed without warning, but it was felt that legal considerations required the issuance of a warrant. That action, of course, ran counter to the US Government's wish that Resolution 837 avoid mentioning Aideed. Issuing a warrant and posting a $25,000 reward for information leading to his capture drove Aideed into hiding and may have boosted his popular standing.[8]

Should Aideed be seen as the hinge on which UNOSOM's success turned? Jonathan Howe became the most prominent advocate of deploying Special Operations Forces. He maintained that capturing Aideed would make "all the difference in the world" and life in the capital would return to normal. Ambassador Robert Gosende, who headed the US Liaison Office in Mogadishu, advised the State Department that he fully agreed. Major General Montgomery also favored deploying SOF because the QRF was not suited to the mission and the allies would not act. He told one of Howe's advisers that Aideed could be captured, but a surgical force was needed to avoid excessive violence.[9] Lieutenant General McCaffrey, Director, J-5, favored supporting the field commanders in Mogadishu who had asked for SOF. General Hoar, however, refused to believe that the key to solving Somalia's problems lay in seizing one man. He rated the chance of capturing Aideed as one in four: a fifty percent chance of getting the necessary intelligence and then a fifty percent chance of actually snaring the warlord, since he would not stay long in one place.[10] General Powell and Secretary Aspin, siding with USCINCCENT, also opposed deploying SOF.

On 14 July, the Deputies Committee directed the Joint Staff to evaluate ways of dealing with Aideed. The J-5 weighed three possibilities: capturing Aideed; "marginalizing" him; or bringing him back into the reconciliation process. The Joint Staff chose "marginalizing" on grounds that Aideed was not "the center of gravity." Its response to the Deputies Committee, circulated on 17 July, recommended (1) giving more emphasis to efforts at political reconciliation and (2) accelerating efforts to pacify Mogadishu and marginalize Aideed. However, capturing Aideed should remain a goal. If a sudden opportunity arose, and Major

General Montgomery felt the circumstances were perfect, the QRF as well as coalition forces were available. Special Operations Forces could reach Mogadishu in forty-eight hours, but keeping them there indefinitely would turn the "UN versus Aideed" battle into a "US versus Aideed" confrontation. The Office of the Secretary of Defense largely adopted the Joint Staff's position. Senior NSC Staff members, however, agreed with Howe and Gosende that Aideed should be arrested and removed from the scene as soon as possible. Deputy National Security Advisor Berger spoke with Under Secretary Wisner and Deputy Secretary of State Peter Tarnoff about moving SOF to Mogadishu. Howe wanted AC-130s, a Marine Expeditionary Unit stationed offshore, and Special Operations Forces. Almost daily, he telephoned Berger, Admiral Jeremiah or General Powell to press the case for deploying SOF. Again, Howe did not offer a concept of operations. At Admiral Jeremiah's suggestion, Howe also requested SOF from the British and Australians, but none were forthcoming.[11]

Between 19 and 27 July an interagency assessment team headed by Ambassador David Shinn, the State Department's coordinator for Somalia, visited Mogadishu and other sites; Colonel Baltimore went as the Joint Staff representative. The team concluded that political and humanitarian activities were not—and must now become—closely integrated with military efforts. UNOSOM needed a comprehensive, detailed plan for restoring Somalia's political institutions. Although the bottom-up approach still appeared sound, UNOSOM seemed to be making largely ad hoc reactions to events. Americans should become less visible in UNOSOM's senior staff posts, but take more mid-level assignments in its political and humanitarian sections. In Mogadishu, the biggest problem stemmed from General Bir's inability to make national contingents follow his orders. The siege mentality that gripped UNOSOM ought to be broken by aggressive, round-the-clock patrolling. Aideed held the initiative and had convinced many Somalis that UNOSOM was militaristic and vengeful. General Montgomery should be given a "short string" to use the QRF (if the opportunity arose) as part of a multinational effort to capture Aideed.[12]

When Secretary Aspin and General Powell met with the Shinn team, Colonel Baltimore delivered the briefing. Powell took deploying SOF and apprehending Aideed to be the team's major recommendations. The Chairman, who still opposed sending SOF, felt that the Shinn team had gone in a direction quite different from the one he had hoped.[13]

The Deputies Committee, with Colonel Baltimore, Rear Admiral Bowman and the Chairman's Assistant, Lieutenant General Michael E. Ryan, USAF, in attendance, reviewed the Shinn team's recommendations on 4 August. It decided that Hoar and Montgomery would assess what SOF capabilities were required for dealing with Aideed, "with an eye toward the US making such capabilities available to UNOSOM." Also, the UN would be pressed to find commercial contractors who would take over logistic tasks being performed by US troops. Finally, a group headed by Ambassador Shinn should start drafting a plan of action for the next six months.[14]

Reconvening on 16 August, the Deputies Committee agreed to implement a four-part plan: first, continue the effort to apprehend Aideed; second, pursue the idea broached by the Ethiopian and Eritrean governments of having clan elders arrange a forced exile for Aideed; third, urge and assist the UN to arrest Aideed's key lieutenants; and fourth, press the UN to prepare detailed plans for Aideed's detention and trial. Thus the Committee explicitly endorsed the view that removing Aideed would "make all the difference" and implicitly moved toward deploying SOF as the way to achieve that goal. The PERT chart [Program, Evaluation and Review Techniques], at this point, was recording the degrees of progress as shown.[15]

Everyone in the Clinton administration agreed that UNOSOM badly needed reinforcements. India had promised a brigade, and Secretary General Boutros-Ghali had asked his native Egypt to supply a second brigade of three thousand men. The Egyptians insisted upon getting one hundred M-113 APCs as a quid pro quo, on grounds that the United States had set a precedent by selling the UN forty M-113s for Pakistan's use. Lieutenant General McCaffrey told Admiral Jeremiah that the price might have to be paid. The Deputies Committee, on 16 August, decided to expedite deployment of the Indian and Pakistani brigades by offering reimbursable lift. One month later, when nothing had moved forward, President Clinton informed Egypt's President Hosni Mubarak that dispatching a brigade "right away would mean a great deal to me." The United States, he promised, would then ship to Egypt replacement equipment "such as APCs."[16] The Egyptians sent forces equivalent to a large battalion, which took over the Mogadishu airfield.

The Debate over "Mission Creep"

Before any more major contingents reached Somalia, the Clinton administration took a small but decisive step to increase US capabilities there. In July, President Clinton had approved dispatch of a team to intercept communications and build a network of informers. Aideed had gone into hiding. Intelligence officers told the Chairman that human intelligence sources were available in Mogadishu but should not be activated unless SOF was on the scene, ready to respond. Powell expressed his belief that these sources were interested only in selling information. They would bring SOF close to Aideed but not to his actual hiding place because, if Aideed were captured, their income would disappear.[17]

In Mogadishu, on 8 August, four US soldiers were killed by a command-detonated mine. Ten days later, intelligence officers reported an ability to acquire "actionable" intelligence. On 19 August, another mine left four US wounded. Faced with renewed requests from field commanders, General Powell reluctantly decided that SOF should be deployed to capture Aideed. He spoke with General Hoar, who reluctantly agreed, and with Lieutenant General McCaffrey, who favored supporting commanders on the scene. "We have to do something," the Chairman then advised Secretary Aspin, "or we are going to be nibbled to death." Secretary Aspin approved the recommendation; President Clinton was informed later. On 22 August, a third land mine explosion wounded six Americans. Three days later, 440 personnel of Task Force Ranger (130 special operations personnel; a company from the Army's 75th Ranger Regiment; 16 helicopters from the Army's special operations aviation unit) arrived in Mogadishu. The number of personnel had been kept as low as possible. Concurrently, the AC-130 gunships were withdrawn. Special Operations Command had only a small number of these planes, and those in Somalia had been little used.[18]

A sense of crisis, going well beyond growing feelings of frustration, gripped the administration. The French and Belgian governments said that they intended to withdraw their contingents at the year's end. General Hoar judged them irreplaceable and warned Powell that their departure could lead to UNOSOM's "progressive deterioration and collapse."[19] Congress was about to reconvene, and even these few US casualties had prompted some members to call for a pullout. The White House had hoped that Howe's appointment would preserve bipartisan support but, by the summer, it became obvious that the administration was doing far more than simply continuing its predecessor's policy. When the Deputies Committee reassembled on 26 August, White House representatives conveyed a great sense of urgency about removing Aideed, deploying the Indian and Egyptian brigades, and organizing a national police force. A day later, Secretary Aspin publicly announced that the QRF would stay until violence in Mogadishu had been quelled, faction leaders surrendered heavy weapons, and a national police force had begun operating in major population centers.[20]

On 1 September, the Somalia Working Group started working upon ways to dissipate Congressional pressure for quick withdrawal. Among other steps, the Joint Staff should examine how best to publicize the completion of contracts that would permit reductions in US logistic personnel. Unfortunately, the J-4 found little evidence of real progress in contracting; the food contract was only a small victory, and a fuels contract was nowhere near completion.

Creating a national police force remained a top priority. Back in July, Jonathan Howe had told the interagency team that it represented "our ticket out of here." Somali policemen seemed to have retained a professional ethic that transcended traditional clan loyalties and made them almost a clan by themselves. The UN had established a rigid requirement that all donations for the police, penal and justice systems must be voluntary. On 16 August, the Deputies Committee decided to use US funds if no other source of funding proved immediately available; none did. But a proposal to provide the force with $25 million in Defense goods and services, along with $6 million from AID funds to help create a judicial system, struck J-4 as poorly conceived. In order to insure proper use of these funds and goods, as many as 550 US personnel (plus their logistic support) would have to go to Somalia. Nonetheless, the Chief Executive on 30 September signed a Presidential Determination directing that $25 million be drawn from Defense commodities and services, and that up to $2 million be furnished from Economic Support Funds. Additionally, AID would provide $6 million for the Somali judicial system.[21] Even so, progress remained almost nonexistent.

Meanwhile, on 4 September, Jonathan Howe decided to try negotiating a forty-eight hour truce with Aideed and the SNA. The next day still another ambush by Aideed's militiamen killed seven Nigerians.[22] On 6 September, through a cable to the State Department, Ambassador Gosende urged a tough response: shelve plans for negotiating a truce; expand Task Force Ranger's mission to include capturing Aideed's lieutenants, and mount a major sweep, using additional forces, into Mogadishu's most troublesome areas. General Hoar disagreed completely, and he immediately told Chairman Powell why. Unless UNOSOM either significantly changed its strategy or dramatically improved its command and control capabilities, Hoar argued, US forces would have to stay indefinitely and incur a "potential for additional mission creep." In Hoar's judgment, UNOSOM had lost control over Mogadishu. Despite repeated warnings that a large-scale infusion of troops was needed, the UN had tried other avenues: wanting to expand into northern and central Somalia, then pursuing facile solutions "like get Aideed and all will be well," and now seeking a reinforced US battalion for sweeps through Mogadishu. In General Hoar's view, sweeps simply would move the weapons around. The Indian contingent, whenever it arrived, would not operate in Mogadishu; the anticipated Egyptian reinforcements would be too few; committing several thousand more US combat troops appeared unacceptable to Congress and the American public. "If the only solution for Mogadishu is large-scale infusion of troops and if the only country available to make this commitment is the US," Hoar concluded, "then it's time to reassess." On 8 September, he sent General Powell an elaboration of his views. The UN was trying to create conditions that had not existed for many years, if ever, and could not be achieved in the near term. Therefore, the United States must either convince the UN to scale back these objectives or significantly increase its own commitment for an indefinite period. Both General Powell and General Hoar kept close watch over Task Force Ranger's operational methods, procedures and tactics. Proposals from the field for Rangers to carry out ambushes, active patrolling, and convoy escort provoked powerful opposition from the Joint Staff.[23]

Under Secretary Wisner shared the fears about mission creep and felt strongly that arms-gathering sweeps, unaccompanied by any political strategy, would prove difficult and possibly pointless. He agreed with an observation by the Chairman that the Horn of Africa was a munitions market; weapons seized today could be replaced tomorrow. (A common joke among UNOSOM personnel was that every Somali carried one weapon and had two or three more in his house). Wisner suggested opening the "fast track" to a peace parley, which would mean power sharing by clan leaders and some warlords. He would let Task Force Ranger continue hunting for Aideed and his lieutenants, but very much opposed sending large-scale reinforcements to help disarm Mogadishu.[24]

The difficulty of regaining control over Mogadishu was vividly illustrated on 9 September, when a US/Pakistani force came under attack from perhaps one thousand Somalis. Helicopter gunships provided suppressive fire, inflicting numerous casualties that probably included participating women and children, because the QRF commander saw no other way to save US troops. Even so, a Pakistani tank and a US bulldozer had to be abandoned. Somali women and children had built obstacles in the road to block escape. Two US soldiers were wounded; the Pakistanis lost one killed and three wounded.

Major General Montgomery felt that UNOSOM was being crippled by continuing friction between the military and the humanitarian/development community. The latter wanted to maintain a neutral, apolitical stance so there was no effective integration of military, political and humanitarian efforts. What should and could be done to turn matters around and revitalize the peacekeeping effort? Repeatedly, at interagency meetings, Admiral Jeremiah asked for a definition of the ultimate US objective or "end state" in Somalia. Updates of the PERT chart contained elaborate matrices designed to show where progress in the security, economic development and institution-building areas was falling short. The chart shown earlier represents where matters were thought to have stood on 17 August. But changing priorities and a host of variables vitiated much of the PERT chart's value. In any case, there was no mechanism for translating what the matrices showed into what the US and especially the UN did. A serious problem, as the Vice Chairman saw it, lay in the fact that the State Department carried out no contingency planning. The NSC Staff, distracted by Bosnia, did not force State to initiate corrective actions when problems were identified. A firm US stance, Jeremiah believed, would have compelled UN headquarters to focus upon attainable goals and drop such early ideas as removing three million mines and redeploying Canadian troops to northern Somalia.[25]

Accommodation with Aideed?

The Deputies Committee, on 11 September, reached a consensus that appeared to back away from the hard line adopted on 26 August and move toward the Hoar-Wisner approach. Militarily, the Committee concluded, UNOSOM ought to concentrate upon pacifying Mogadishu. Politically, the "bottom up" approach should be replaced by an accelerated effort to achieve reconciliation among the warlords. US forces would still help any UNOSOM contingents that got into trouble, however, and would keep trying to apprehend Aideed and his lieutenants.[26] Abandonment of the "bottom up" approach was no doubt realistic. Still, it is singular that a strategy that the NSC had endorsed, and on which considerable effort had been expended, should have been replaced by the Deputies in such a quick and seemingly casual manner.

There was a multiplicity of views in the field as well as in Washington. General Hoar apparently anticipated that UNOSOM would fail to carry out its mandate and wanted to limit damage to the United States. Jonathan Howe, who held a UN post but exploited his ties with top US officials to the utmost, despised Aideed and believed that eliminating him would vastly ease problems of political reconstruction. Ambassador Gosende, who also detested Aideed, looked for ways to achieve Howe's objective while backing away from some of Howe's confrontational methods.

When General Hoar visited Mogadishu on 9 September and met Ambassador Gosende, he repeated his view that additional US forces would not solve Somalia's problem. Gosende agreed on that point. The alternatives, Gosende continued, were to either find other forces or get out. But the Ambassador advocated activism, believing that a turning point had come and that a UN failure would damage US leadership worldwide. Hoar, conversely, held that the UN already had fallen down in the most basic tasks of supporting UNOSOM II.[27]

On 15 September, through a letter to Assistant Secretary of State George Moose, Ambassador Gosende spelled out his differences with General Hoar. He disputed Hoar's claim that there were fundamental divergences between the objectives set forth in Secretary Aspin's speech of 27 August and those in Security Council Resolution 814. Gosende pointedly recalled that "every phrase, period and comma" of Resolution 814 had been carefully coordinated within the US government. At that time, he added, the USCENTCOM staff had been only too happy to hand over to UNOSOM missions like political reconciliation and creation of a national police force. After his recent visit to Mogadishu, General Hoar had limited the QRF's role to "force protection"; Gosende believed that Aideed and other warlords soon would perceive that UNOSOM had lost its teeth. Hoar claimed that nationally imposed limitations were the main obstacles to effective UN peacekeeping operations. Ambassador Gosende agreed, but added that the most far-reaching limitations were being imposed by USCENTCOM headquarters in Tampa and by Washington.[28]

Nonetheless, support for a policy that would stress compromise more than confrontation seemed to be gaining momentum. On 16 September, the Office of the Assistant Secretary of Defense (Regional Security Affairs) recommended pressing the UN to emphasize a political instead of a military strategy: negotiate a cease-fire, then form a transitional national council; starting 1 November, use the QRF only for emergencies during limited periods; and by 1 January 1994, replace the US QRF with a foreign contingent. Next day, after reviewing this draft, the Director, J-5, advised General Powell that the QRF should remain to protect US forces. As for Aideed, Lieutenant General McCaffrey favored continuing an aggressive hunt without "personalizing" the conflict. He did not specify how the distinction would be drawn.[29]

Ambassador Gosende suggested another way to get off "dead center": establish a ten-man UN commission, with two Habr Gidr elders, to investigate the 5 June incident. Aideed would go into a period of exile; the SNA would agree to a cease-fire, cantonment of heavy weapons, and demobilization of militia. Aideed's rejection of this offer, argued the Ambassador, would alienate many of his clansmen and make it much easier to apprehend Aideed and his lieutenants. Gosende's proposal, cabled to the State Department on 18 September, flowed from a conviction that the United States was not willing to commit enough manpower and political capital to destroy Aideed.[30]

The State Department did not reply directly. But a "non-paper," which Secretary Christopher gave to Boutros-Ghali on 20 September, incorporated a good part of Ambassador Gosende's views. The "bottom up" approach, it argued, could not succeed quickly enough to satisfy the US Congress and public. Therefore, the time had come to seek a cease-fire, create an interim governing authority, and open a dialogue with Aideed aimed at persuading him to leave Somalia. The QRF should move back "over the horizon" as soon as possible; rangers could leave once Aideed ceased being a problem, and contractors could take over some US functions after Mogadishu became secure. The Vice Director, J-2, detected some weaknesses in the "non-paper." Aideed was being given no real incentive to leave Somalia, and what would happen if he resolved to stay? Moreover, an accommodation with Aideed would make him "the national strongman—a winner": "This is one way to get out of Somalia if we have no illusions about the outcome."

The Secretary General had no intention of letting Aideed emerge as a winner. Boutros-Ghali did ask Special Envoy Howe to examine the feasibility of establishing an interim government. But he told Secretary Christopher, on 25 September, that Aideed must be either neutralized or brought to justice and that the factions must be disarmed. Until those things were done, Boutros-Ghali said that he opposed withdrawing the QRF.[31]

Ambassador Gosende agreed that, if US troops were limited to force protection, a cease-fire should be negotiated as quickly as possible. On 27 September, USCINCCENT told the Chairman that he favored negotiating with the Habr Gidr subclan, although not with Aideed personally. General Hoar assumed that Aideed would continue to elude capture and, much like Gosende, suggested either creating a study commission and offering Aideed safe haven in another country or as a last resort ending Aideed's outlaw status to achieve reconciliation. Once again, Hoar urged a coordinated effort—political, humanitarian and psychological as well as military—to regain control of Mogadishu. He looked upon the QRF as the linch-pin of the whole coalition and rated helicopter gunships as the QRF's truly indis-pensable element. The South Koreans might be enticed into providing the QRF, if an amphibious ready group with embarked Marines stayed in Somali waters for several months.[32]

Patience was running out fast on Capitol Hill. Each firefight prompted more Congressional calls for a prompt US pullout. Republicans had been criticizing administration policy for several months, and now considerable numbers of Democrats joined them.[33] On 28 September, Lieutenant General McCaffrey sent General Powell an appraisal of how US withdrawal would affect UNOSOM:

1. Withdrawing in 45 days, by 15 November, would create a high probability that UNOSOM would cease being viable and a rapid exodus of contributors would follow.

2. Withdrawing in 90 days, by 1 January 1994, would leave a medium to low probability that UNOSOM would stay viable. There seemed a reasonable possibility of avoiding the stark characterization that departure was a tacti-cal defeat brought about by Aideed.

3. Withdrawing in 180 days, by 1 April 1994, would remain consistent with U.S. commitments and offer a reasonable probability of keeping UNOSOM successfully engaged.

The very next day, 29 September, saw Senate passage of a nonbinding "sense of Congress" resolution that by 15 November President Clinton should seek and obtain authorization for the US deployment to continue.[34]

Had a major policy shift already taken place? On 25 September, during a White House meeting about Bosnia, General Powell recommended either sending rein-forcements to Somalia or changing the policy.[35] Two days later, administration spokesmen did say publicly that the US government had moved away from its goal of capturing Aideed and was focusing instead upon isolating the warlord and creat-ing a political structure without him.[36] But the available evidence shows no deter-mination to carry out a clear-cut change. Somalia continued as an agenda topic among NSC principals. However, after President Clinton signed PDD-5 [presiden-tial decision directive] in May, review of policy options and formulation of guid-ance were done in the Deputies Committee. What came out of the Deputies Com-mittee's meetings was a series of incremental adjustments, occasionally inconsistent and sometimes so finely nuanced that lower levels either did not interpret them as major changes or could not translate them into concrete actions.[37] The PCC and DC were not intended to be decision-making bodies, and their decisions frequently reflected either consensus or lowest common denominator compromises. Ambiguity and improvisation continued to characterize the policymaking process. The upshot was that when the United States took sides in Somalia's civil war, it chose an enemy but never could find an acceptable ally—and even if it had, that ally would have become just another faction.

Within the Pentagon, still another reappraisal had started, evidently driven by domestic political considerations. Secretary Aspin instructed a long-time associate, Mr. Clark Murdock, to attend some meetings of the Somalia Working Group and devise an "exit strategy." When Mr. Murdock did so, during the week of 27 September, he felt that Group members were much more pessimistic than the Principals had been given to understand. He then told them that the PERT chart's three-track strategy was unrealistic, that things were going badly in Somalia, that the US should "bug out," and that he intended to send the Secretary a report saying so.[38] Rear Admiral Bowman also had become part of a general consensus that the time had come to change course.[39] He met with Joint Staff officers on Friday, 1 October, and gave them guidance for drafting a new strategy paper. Action officers still assumed, though, that the three-track strategy in the PERT chart portrayed US policy objectives. They worked through the weekend and were distributing their final report on Sunday, 3 October, when word of a bloody firefight in Mogadishu reached the National Military Command Center (NMCC).

Meantime, US commanders in Somalia had not received any new guidance from USCENTCOM, so the fight against Aideed went on. As a practical matter, there was no middle ground; the warlord had to be either hunted down or accepted back. On 7 September, in fact, Task Force Ranger put emphasis on hunting six of Aideed's lieutenants. Jonathan Howe later recalled being told, as late as 23 September, that SOF commanders still were optimistic about capturing Aideed.[40] Meanwhile, in mid-August, Major General Montgomery had sent USCINCCENT a request for a mechanized task force as well as an air cavalry troop. General Hoar visited Mogadishu in September and said that such a request "would not fly politically." On 14 September, Montgomery informed USCINCCENT that he wanted a tank platoon with four M-1 tanks, a mechanized company with 14 Bradley M-2 IFVs, and an artillery battery with six 105 mm. howitzers. Minings, mortar attacks and ambushes had led him to conclude that heavy forces were needed to protect US logistics convoys and installations in and around Mogadi-shu. On 21 September, Task Force Ranger captured one of Aideed's most promi-nent lieutenants, Osman Ato. Next day, USCINCCENT told General Powell that he favored sending the tank platoon and the mechanized company but not the artillery battery. General Hoar also noted potential drawbacks to deploying more units: elevating Aideed's stature; enlarging the US "footprint" in UNOSOM; and increasing the potential for collateral damage. General McCaffrey later remem-bered arguing repeatedly in conversations with Generals Powell, Hoar and Mont-gomery, for the deployment of armor. McCaffrey also recalled warning Under Secretary Wisner that, without armor and artillery reinforcements, he foresaw a disaster with one hundred US casualties and ten missing in action. On 23 Septem-ber, Chairman Powell discussed USCINCCENT's request with the Service Chiefs and particularly with the Army Chief of Staff, General Gordon R. Sullivan, who endorsed it. Powell then told Secretary Aspin that it had his support as well. The Secretary did not approve, however, on grounds that "the trend is going the other way" and that Congressional critics would berate the administration. At General Hoar's urging, the Chairman repeated his request very soon afterward and the Secretary again did not act upon it. USCINCCENT raised Montgomery's request with the Chairman three times between 22 and 30 September. Powell's last day as Chairman was 30 September. When he paid his farewell call on the President, the two men stood on the Truman balcony of the White House; General Powell told President Clinton that the situation in Somalia was unraveling and urged that all US and UN troops be withdrawn.[41]

A Bloody Raid Forces a Decision to Withdraw

On the afternoon of 3 October, Task Force Ranger launched a raid that met unexpectedly strong resistance, produced a long list of US casualties, and turned Congress decisively against staying in Somalia. At 1540 hours, the Rangers stormed a building near Mogadishu's Olympic Hotel and apprehended twenty-four of Aideed's henchmen. But forty minutes later, as the Rangers prepared to leave by truck convoy, rocket-propelled grenades hit and downed a US helicopter. About ninety men of Task Force Ranger moved to and formed a perimeter around the wrecked helicopter, where swarms of Somali militia pinned them down. Then a second helicopter was hit and crashed two miles away; Somali militia eventually overran this site. A small relief column set out from the airport but had to pull back; so did a QRF company from the 10th Mountain Division. Major General

Montgomery ordered the QRF, which already was on the move, to assemble a battalion-size force at the airport. He also requested all the Pakistani M-48 tanks—four of eight proved operational—and twenty-eight M-113s from Malaysians who made up UNOSOM's QRF. This was a more deliberate effort to rescue the Rangers and hold down losses in the relief force. Task Force Ranger was being supplied by air, but it remained pinned down. A seventy-vehicle column, with US troops aboard the Malaysian armored personnel carriers (APCs), did not get under way until 2315. The force battled through strong resistance; two Malaysian soldiers were killed. Relief forces finally reached the crash sites around 0230 hours, but not until 0700 hours, after remains had been removed from a crashed helicopter, did all the men of Task Force Ranger make their way to safety. American casualties in Task Force Ranger and the QRF came to eighteen killed and eighty-four wounded; one helicopter pilot was held captive for eleven days. The Somalis claimed to have suffered 312 dead and 814 wounded.[42]

Just as the grim news from Mogadishu reached Washington on Sunday afternoon, 3 October, a Joint Staff team led by J-5 completed the paper commissioned by Rear Admiral Bowman two days earlier. In it, they recommended withdrawing the majority of US forces by 31 March 1994. The team proposed (1) rapidly arranging a cease-fire with the Habr Gidr clan "while bringing Aideed into domestic arrest or foreign exile and investigation," (2) pressing efforts, which had been ineffectual so far, to establish a national police force and a judicial system, (3) raising UNOSOM's strength from 26,000 to 28-32,000 by bringing in Egyptian, Indian and Pakistani reinforcements, (4) replacing US logistic troops with contractors as well as with other countries' military units, and (5) restricting the QRF's role, moving it over the horizon after US logistic troops departed.[43] A few weeks earlier, these recommendations might have made a significant impact. Now, the main ones seemed overtaken by events.

Among themselves, senior civilians in the Pentagon wondered why the Rangers made this raid six days after administration spokesmen had said that the US goal now was to isolate Aideed, not capture him. They felt the military should have reacted to this policy change, and speculated that the NSC Staff probably assumed new guidance would be sent to the field.[44] It must be emphasized, though, that Joint Staff officers did not believe that any policy change had been promulgated. To them and to Major General Montgomery as well, "marginalizing" or isolating Aideed remained the constant policy and maintaining military pressure was a subset of it. Thus the 3 October Joint Staff paper proposed bringing

Aideed "into domestic arrest or foreign exile and investigation." Recalling how the hint of a forty-eight hour truce had been followed immediately by an ambush of Nigerian peacekeepers, Joint Staff officers were convinced that Aideed would respond only to unrelenting military pressure. Similarly, they saw Ambassador Gosende's cable of 18 September not as a bid to change policy but as an attempt to re-energize the political track of the three-track strategy. Gosende was disappointed that his cable evoked no reply from the State Department and he too assumed that the policy remained the same.[45]

In any event, the Clinton administration faced a firestorm of criticism from Congress. Televised pictures of a dead American being dragged through Mogadishu's streets fuelled popular revulsion against staying in Somalia. Secretary Aspin, in particular, came under attack for having refused to send the M-1 tanks and M-2 Bradley IFVs. Generals Hoar and Montgomery, in testimony before the Senate Armed Services Committee, gave their opinion that M-1s and M-2s would have reached embattled Rangers faster than the Pakistani M-48s and Malaysian M-113s. Ranger casualties probably would have been the same, they said, but a QRF force equipped with M-1s might have avoided any losses.[46] This episode was widely interpreted as having contributed to President Clinton's decision, announced on 15 December, that Aspin would be leaving OSD.

Public pressure was such that, immediately after the 3 October raid, President Clinton felt he had to safeguard forces on the ground and to decide exactly when the US military presence in Somalia would end.[47] The NSC started issuing tasking directives at once, without awaiting military input. On 3 October, US forces in Somalia totaled about 4,650 personnel: 1,450 in the QRF; 450 in the Joint Special Operations Task Force; and 2,600 in logistic support units. Four OH-58D helicopters were flown into Mogadishu on 4 October. Next day, two helicopter gunships arrived and two AC-130 gunships flew from Italy to Mombassa, Kenya. In the Pentagon the Director, J-3, was temporarily absent on 3 October and Lieutenant General McCaffrey stepped in, which briefly created a jurisdictional issue. Initially, Admiral Jeremiah and the J-3 recommended sending two carrier battle groups and two amphibious ready groups, which would take several weeks to reach Mogadishu. McCaffrey pushed for prompt F-15 and B-52 strikes against equipment storage sites, and immediate shipborne deployment of a heavy brigade.[48] On 5 October, the J-3 drew up US reinforcement options: a "light" package of 970 personnel that included a mechanized battalion task force and a mechanized company team; a "medium" one with 2,900 personnel, including a light infantry battalion, two mechanized task forces, one aviation lift and one aviation attack company; and a "heavy" package comprising a 12,000- strong light infantry division.

There were almost continuous meetings over several days at various levels, and coordination was not always attained. Admiral Jeremiah held several telephone conversations with General Hoar; the two men spent six hours at the White House reviewing options with President Clinton. Jeremiah then talked to the Chief Executive alone. President Clinton voiced concern about criticism from Congress; providing more protection meant risking more casualties. Admiral Jeremiah proposed deploying carrier-based aircraft and Marine amphibious forces; Somalis knew what the planes could do and respected the Marines. The key point was that some US forces would be immediately available but offshore and thus immune from risk, except when landed and actively engaged. Clinton agreed.

Speaking to the nation on 7 October, President Clinton announced that 1,700 Army troops with 104 armored vehicles would deploy to Somalia and stay under US command. Additionally, the carrier, USS *Abraham Lincoln,* as well as two amphibious ready groups with thirty-six hundred Marines would be stationed offshore. By 31 March 1994, Clinton promised, all US troops would be gone from Somalia "except for a few hundred support personnel in non-combat roles." He now defined the US mission as four-fold. First, "protect our troops and our bases...." Second, keep open and secure the roads, port and lines of communication essential for the flow of relief supplies. Third, "keep the pressure on those who cut off relief supplies and attack our people, not to personalize the conflict but to prevent a return to anarchy." Fourth, "help make it possible for the Somali people ... to reach agreement among themselves...."[49]

On 8 October, Lieutenant General McCaffrey sent Admiral Jeremiah recommendations about how to carry out the mission that President Clinton had just defined:

1. As an absolute prerequisite to the success of reconciliation efforts, rapidly recruit more troops for UNOSOM. Pakistan should be the prime target, Egypt next, and then South Korea as a source for the QRF. The United States would have to provide transportation and equipment, and even pay operating costs. Teams dedicated solely to recruitment should be formed in J-5, OSD, the State Department, and the US Delegation to the United Nations.

2. Press for a cease-fire, political reconciliation, and creation of a transitional governmental authority. The President's reappointment of Robert Oakley

as his Special Envoy would allow the United States, not the United Nations and Jonathan Howe, to direct developments.

3. Revitalize the effort to create a national police force by appointing a US official, complemented by a UN officer in Somalia, who would have sufficient authority and resources.

4. Prepare to have civilians replace US logistic troops. Since the Joint Staff and OSD would work directly with contractors, McCaffrey predicted that this would be one of the more efficiently executed parts of the enterprise.[50] His forecast was quite accurate. Of the four areas, logistics proved to be the only one in which any real progress occurred.

Five task forces on Somalia, each headed by an Assistant Secretary or a three-star officer, were set up. The five chairmen constituted an Executive Committee on Somalia. Lieutenant General McCaffrey chaired the task force on logistics transition. On 4 October, Lieutenant Colonel Gordon Kennedy, USA, from the International Logistics Division, J-4, led a team to UN headquarters in New York. He kept in daily contact with Colonel James M. Colvin, Jr., USA, in J-4. A UN logistics cell, about forty strong, had been moved into the new UN Department of Peacekeeping Operations. Two weeks later, despite President Clinton's announcement of a withdrawal deadline, the UN had done nothing. Lieutenant Colonel Kennedy then prepared an options paper for the UN logistics cell. United Nations officials would have preferred to write a series of small contracts, but UNOSOM lacked the field personnel to manage them. Consequently, Kennedy pressed for one "umbrella" contract. The only way to continue functions being performed by US Army logistic units was to extend and expand the existing contract with a private firm, Brown and Root. Funds could be provided to Brown and Root through either a unilateral US contract or a UN Letter of Assist. The UN would ask about cost and availability; the US government specified prices and services. The UN then confirmed by a Letter of Assist that it would pay.

On 30 October, Lieutenant General McCaffrey spoke with Secretary General Boutros-Ghali about promptly completing a Letter of Assist and, by 15 November, providing Brown and Root with $50 million in "seed money." Two days later, when the Executive Committee convened, the Vice Director, J-5, asked for OSD's help in drafting legislation to fund a contract; the UN bureaucracy's past performance created worry that a Letter of Assist would be delayed. On 5 November, Joint Staff, Army and UN representatives drafted a Statement of Work. It was decided that the US Army's twenty-three logistic support units in Somalia would lease $43 million worth of equipment to Brown and Root; the Director, Joint Staff, so informed USCINCCENT. On 10 November, the UN Contracts Committee accepted a US proposal and the Letter of Assist was issued. Nine days later, a contract for support through 31 March was signed. Brown and Root would take over all logistic functions by 15 January; Army Forces Command, acting as USCENT-COM's Army component, would arrange for the Bangladeshi battalion at Mogadishu to provide security for Brown and Root logistic operations.

United Nations officials felt the contract was overpriced and gave the United States too large a role just when US troops were leaving. The cost may have been excessive, but US officials countered that time was of the essence and UNOSOM could be kept viable only by working through the US government, which dealt with Brown and Root. On 1 December, General John M. Shalikashvili, USA, the new Chairman of the Joint Chiefs of Staff, told Under Secretary General Annan that US equipment leased to Brown and Root must be returned when the contract expired on 31 March. The Chairman suggested, though, that some items could remain if the UN requested them. A much larger amount of US equipment was sold, rather than leased, to the UN.[51]

Meanwhile, on 10 October, Aideed had declared a unilateral cease-fire. His militia had been hurt badly in the battle with Task Force Ranger. Five days later, USCINCCENT sent Major General Montgomery a statement of Commander's Intent: Minimize US, UN and Somali casualties while supporting efforts to find a political solution. The protection of US forces, which included launching pre-emptive defensive strikes, remained the priority mission. Military operations would not expand beyond those limits unless doing so would contribute to a political solution. Any offensive operations (i.e., unprovoked attacks against installations, logistic sites and arms caches) would have to be approved in advance by the National Command Authority. On 19 October, the President ordered that Army Rangers be withdrawn from Somalia.

Joint Task Force Somalia, commanded by Major General Carl F. Ernst, USA, was activated on 20 October. Its mission was four-fold: first and foremost, protect US forces; second, support UNOSOM II's operations, which meant that JTF Somalia functioned as the QRF; third, as required, secure lines of communication to ensure the continued flow of relief supplies; and fourth, prepare for the withdrawal of US forces. JTF Somalia came under the tactical control of Major General Montgomery as COMUSFORSOMALIA. However, Ernst had 180 personnel in his headquarters while Montgomery had only about 40 in his, plus 15 individuals assigned to the UNOSOM command staff that he used for US operations as well. Although General Hoar wanted to distance US from UN activities, Montgomery's staff worked out of the US Logistical Support Command that was dedicated to supporting UNOSOM II. Consequently, JTF Somalia remained separate from UNOSOM and conducted detailed operational planning but reported to Major General Montgomery who had only a tiny staff and functioned mainly in a UNOSOM role. In these circumstances, some degree of misperception between Generals Ernst and Montgomery proved unavoidable. Montgomery expected JTF Somalia to protect US logistical bases and convoys, but the JTF staff drafted a campaign plan for possibly re-establishing UNOSOM's control throughout Somalia.[52]

Liquidation

On 9 November, USCINCCENT sent General Shalikashvili and Secretary Aspin a four-phase plan for withdrawing:

1. Make withdrawal preparations; enhance the capabilities of air and sea points of exit.

2. By 31 December, reduce US forces ashore to 5-6,000 and transfer most logistic support functions to Brown and Root.

3. By early March, complete the transfer of logistic support functions, and give the QRF role to UN forces.

4. Complete withdrawal by 31 March.

This plan, which was approved and promulgated on 28 November assumed that the cease-fire would hold and that 10-15,000 UN troops would remain in Somalia. Already, though, the US Liaison Office had warned that UNOSOM "while still nominally intact, is mentally unraveling." Other contributing countries felt they were in Somalia because the United States had pressed them to come. Why should they run risks that the United States appeared unwilling to take?[53]

Early in November, UNOSOM's main combat elements were: one Egyptian and two Pakistani brigades as well as Bangladeshi, Malaysian, Nepalese, Nigerian, Saudi Arabian and United Arab Emirate battalions in and around Mogadishu; one Italian brigade at nearby Gialalassi; and one newly-arrived Indian brigade at Baidoa. UNOSOM's viability seemed to depend largely upon whether the Egyptian and Pakistani contingents remained. On 9 November, the Egyptian government asked the United States for 213 M-113 APCs and more than 400 other vehicles. The administration decided to supply seventy M-113s and nothing more. Pakistan requested 30 tanks, 80 APCs, and 150 vehicles.[54]

The UN Security Council on 16 November, through Resolution 886, established a Commission of Inquiry to investigate the 5 June attack; this action effectively ended the hunt for Aideed. Concurrently, however, UNOSOM Headquarters concluded that Aideed probably intended to resume fighting at some later time because a peaceful resolution would not serve his interests. Richard Clarke of the NSC Staff reacted by asking members of the Somalia Executive Committee to assess where matters seemed to be heading. The J-5 prepared an assessment that the UN humanitarian effort was too passive, that political reconciliation had not advanced appreciably, and that Somalis no longer took UNOSOM's military presence seriously. The administration should either take "aggressive action" to enhance UNOSOM's credibility after US forces withdrew or, failing that, end the UN mandate and bring coalition partners home by 31 March. The J-5 advocated an intensive media campaign declaring UNOSOM's primary mission a success because starvation had been stopped, and placing Somalia's future squarely in the hands of its people.[55]

There was now a surfeit of senior American civilians in Mogadishu: Jonathan Howe, who reported to Boutros-Ghali; Robert Oakley, who reported to President Clinton; and Richard Bogosian, who replaced Robert Gosende at the US Liaison Office. Guidance from them sometimes appeared contradictory. Ambassador Oakley told Major General Montgomery not to provoke the SNA by test-firing AC-130s within earshot of Mogadishu, but then encouraged Major General Ernst to prepare a plan for reopening 21 October Road. On 16 November, Ambassador Bogosian conferred with Lieutenant General Bir. Bir wanted UNOSOM troops to start depending on voluntary cooperation from the clans and use force only in self-defense. Even without US participation, Bir believed that a sixteen thousand-man UN force could remain viable by refocusing its mission away from security to political and humanitarian goals.

Although more UN troops were in Mogadishu by October than had been there in May, security was worse. Clearly, however, Aideed had been impressed by JTF Somalia's show of strength. The test came over whether US and UN forces would reopen 21 October Road, along which SNA militia had set up more than a dozen roadblocks. This three-lane avenue running through Mogadishu was the main supply route to the north; the alternative, a bypass road, consisted of one dirt lane each way and added one hundred kilometers to the route. JTF Somalia, working with the Pakistanis, planned a UN operation to reopen 21 October Road; US intelligence believed that the SNA would not fight. About 20 November, Major General Ernst briefed Lieutenant General James R. Ellis, USA, Commanding General, Third Army, who was visiting. Ellis then went to UNOSOM Headquarters, where he was told that Headquarters had decided against clearing the road because of anticipated casualties. On 25 November, Major General Montgomery told Ambassador Bogosian that no offensive operations were envisioned and that such action probably would require presidential approval. In fact, Montgomery saw no military necessity to reopen 21 October Road as long as the bypass, which had been improved by UNOSOM engineers, remained usable. Ernst said later that the SNA militia, realizing that neither JTF Somalia nor UNOSOM II would take the offensive, soon recaptured the initiative in Mogadishu.[56]

Major General Montgomery felt that UNOSOM II had lost the initiative on 7 October, when President Clinton announced a withdrawal deadline. He considered his guidance very narrow and excluding any offensive maneuver. Montgomery rated JTF Somalia a success simply because it deterred any SNA interference with the US withdrawal.[57]

The path of reconciliation led to Aideed's emergence as a "winner," as the J-2 had foreseen. Ambassador Oakley spoke to SNA representatives who made clear that Aideed would not negotiate with UNOSOM until the arrest warrant had been lifted and his lieutenants released. Privately, Americans referred to these SNA spokesmen as "the North Koreans of Somalia." The warrant on Aideed was withdrawn, but General Hoar felt that eight of the thirty-nine detainees, who were directly linked to the 5 June ambush, should remain in confinement. Those eight stayed in custody although, at White House meetings in late November, it became apparent that high officials did not know why the men were still being held.[58] But Aideed and the Americans both wanted progress toward a political settlement, albeit for different reasons. So on 2 December a US Army C-12 aircraft, which supported Ambassador Oakley, flew Aideed to Ethiopia for reconciliation talks with rival clan leaders. Since Aideed would neither board a UN aircraft nor share a plane with Ali Mahdi, Oakley decided to let him use the C-12.

Concurrently, the Deputies Committee decided to look favorably upon a strategy, advocated by the NSC Staff and the State Department, of decentralizing UNOSOM's activities. Operations in Mogadishu would be deemphasized and activities shifted to other cities. For example, UNOSOM headquarters would move to Baledogle, US equipment would be distributed among outlying police units, and local councils would receive bloc aid grants. The J-5, on 6 December, described decentralization as an "intriguing" concept but observed that no US forces were available to support additional projects. The 43rd Engineer Battalion, the only such US unit in Somalia, was due to depart on 18 December. Without political reconciliation, J-5 continued, decentralization would place dispersed UN forces at significant risk. But if reconciliation came about, decentralization would be unnecessary. The Somalia Executive Committee also discussed whether to rely on other ports instead of Mogadishu. The J-4, however, concluded that three to six months would be needed to restore Kismayo, five months for the Old Port of Mogadishu. In any case, Mogadishu's port and airfield still would remain necessary to evacuate US and UNOSOM contingents.[59]

The NSC Staff and the State Department felt that decentralization offered the best chance of marginalizing uncooperative Somalis, because only secure regions would receive humanitarian support. Ambassador Oakley, on 9 December, advised the Somalia Executive Committee that decentralization ultimately would fail without political reconciliation and accompanying security guarantees. Just after Christmas, Jonathan Howe told the Acting Secretary of State that decentralization outside Mogadishu was largely ephemeral and described the UN's slowness in moving to organize a national police force as scandalous.[60]

The 31 March deadline meant that two decisions about US forces had to be made: How would units withdraw, and how few personnel ought to remain? Unconfirmed intelligence reports indicated that Somalis possessed shoulder-fired SA-7 surface-to-air missiles. Planes leaving Mogadishu airport would be vulnerable, and the administration did not want to run the slightest risk of substantial casualties. General Shalikashvili discussed the matter with Major General Montgomery during a visit to Mogadishu on 20-21 December, and then with General Hoar early in January. Accordingly, SS *Empire State* and the motor vessel *Mediterranean Sky* took troops aboard at Mogadishu and steamed to Mombassa, Kenya, where troops switched to commercial aircraft and flew home.

As to a residual presence, US personnel occupied forty-three billets on the UNOSOM staff; the UN asked that twelve billets be filled after 31 March. The NSC Staff and the State Department favored leaving enough US personnel to influence events and ensure that the UNOSOM staff kept functioning. But OSD, the Joint Staff, General Montgomery and USCINCCENT advocated leaving only the minimum required to support the US Liaison Office. As Montgomery put it, a few personnel were not critical; the time had come for others to carry the load.[61] Twelve officers from all Services were assigned to serve in the Logistic Support Center on UNOSOM's civilian side.

In mid-January 1994, the Deputies Committee decided that the United States would remain actively engaged in Somalia. That meant assisting a large police/ justice program as well as a sizable rehabilitation effort, requiring greater Somali responsibility and threatening an aid cutoff if progress did not occur. But the seven thousand police were poorly equipped, unevenly distributed throughout the country, and lacked direction. Moreover, UNOSOM's police component had no planners, no operations officers, and no accountants. Commander William Stettinius, USN, who was assigned to Regional Security Affairs, OSD, went to Somalia as an adviser on police issues. At his advice and that of an Australian, Bill Kirk, the UNOSOM Force Commander instructed area commanders to oversee the police. However, the SNA refused to deal with Stettinius in his UNOSOM capacity and held that no equipment should be distributed until a truly national police force had been formed. Shipment from US ports of $25 million worth of US equipment, principally trucks, rifles and sidearms, was under way. Stettinius assured SNA representatives that equipment being positioned around the country would not be distributed until a police structure was put in place—and that never happened.[62]

Each week, Somalia seemed to unravel a little more. The UN released the last detainees, including Osman Ato, on 18 January. Major General Montgomery stepped down as Deputy UNOSOM Force Commander on 7 February. "It's time to get out," he declared publicly. "At some point in time you've got to stand up and take responsibility, and Somalis will not take responsibility." Concurrently, UN headquarters announced that Jonathan Howe's tour as Special Representative would end. By early March, security in Mogadishu had deteriorated so badly that Ambassador Bogosian recommended threatening to close the Liaison Office and end all US assistance unless Somali factions quickly proved they could make peace and restore order. During 12-13 March, General Shalikashvili visited Mogadishu and conferred with US military and civilian officials. What, the Chairman asked, were the chances of US and UN failure? Even if the United States ended its efforts and famine returned, he remarked, the original mission still could be regarded as a success. Ambassador Bogosian said that UNOSOM would collapse without US support; participation should continue as long as progress was discernible. General Montgomery, who was overseeing the US pullout, argued that

Marines were lightning rods. If some stayed as security officers, the administration must be prepared for casualties. The Chairman stated his "gut feeling" that the administration would rather not evacuate. Deputy Under Secretary of Defense Walter Slocombe commented that the administration also would rather not see any more casualties.[63]

The last eleven hundred US Marines left Mogadishu on 25 March. By then, French, German, Belgian, Italian, Turkish and Tunisian contingents also had withdrawn. UNOSOM's strength totaled about 20,000, consisting mainly of 7,220 Pakistanis with QRF responsibility, 1,660 Egyptians in Mogadishu, and 4,930 Indians at Kismayo and Bardera. Meantime, Aideed and Ali Mahdi met at Nairobi, Kenya, and signed an agreement on broad principles for reconciliation and reconstruction. The accord proved short-lived and probably was a ploy to keep US aid flowing. UNOSOM quickly proved impotent in the face of renewed clan warfare. The warlords aimed at seizing UN stockpiles, mostly supplied by the United States, and even at disarming UNOSOM contingents. A Zimbabwean company, for instance, was surrounded and forced to surrender all its weapons and equipment. Egyptians were told that militias would let them evacuate from Mogadishu unopposed only if they left all their equipment behind. By summer, the US government was urging the UN to end its mandate. When the US Liaison Office closed and its 55 Marine guards were evacuated on 19 September, Somalia had reverted to a political state not far from the anarchy of 1992.

Conclusion

For the United States, the cost came to 32 killed in action, 172 wounded and $1.3 billion spent through 30 June 1994. The effort in Somalia succeeded as a short-term humanitarian mission but then failed as an attempt at nation-building and as an international venture in peace enforcement. Even at the outset of Operation RESTORE HOPE, there were those who foresaw the final outcome. On 1 December 1992, just before the first US Marines landed at Mogadishu, Ambassador Smith Hempstone sent the State Department a cable titled "The Somali Tarbaby" that proved remarkably prescient:

> Somalis ... are natural-born guerrillas. They will mine the roads. They will lay ambushes. They will launch hit-and-run attacks.... If you liked Beirut, you'll love Mogadishu.
> To what end? To keep tens of thousands of Somali kids from starving to death in 1993 who, in all probability, will starve to death in 1994 (unless we are prepared to remain through 1994)? ... I have heard estimates ... that it will take five years to get Somalia not on its feet but just on its knees....
> Finally, what will we leave behind when we depart? The Somali is treacherous. The Somali is a killer. The Somali is as tough as his country, and just as unforgiving....
> We ought to have learned by now that these situations are easier to get into than to get out of, that no good deed goes unpunished.[1]

The Joint Staff's attitude, while never so pungently phrased, was roughly the same as Ambassador Hempstone's, opposing the decision to carry out a major ground intervention in November 1992. Joint Staff officers did experience short periods of hope, during the early phase of UNITAF and later when the police project seemed about to move forward, but skepticism was the more frequent sentiment. General Powell came to favor large-scale intervention but strictly for humanitarian relief objectives. During the summer of 1993, he rejected recommendations from the Director, J-5, and the Shinn team to deploy SOF and hunt Aideed. The Chairman changed his position late in August only after American soldiers had been targets in three ambushes, then he concluded within a month that the enterprise was failing and that US and UN troops should withdraw.

The US objective in Somalia proved to be a constantly shifting target. Somalia was a frequent agenda and discussion topic for the President and his senior advisors, but for the months between November 1992 when President Bush decided to intervene and October 1993 when President Clinton decided to pull out, imprecision and drift often reigned. Discussions in the Deputies Committee, where guidance was formulated, came to revolve around short-term tactics without reference to long-term objectives. Steps that General Hoar condemned as "mission creep" really depended on how and by whom the mission was being defined at that moment. Those who advocated deploying SOF relied upon the maxim of fighting to win. General Powell wanted to keep objectives limited, which meant minimizing US military involvement. His change of mind about using SOF came in response to ambushes of US troops, not as part of a broad policy reconsideration. Within two weeks after the SOF reached Mogadishu, some who had advocated its deployment began calling for an accommodation with Aideed. Yet hindsight suggests that every change of tactics only reduced policy-makers' maneuver room and made UNOSOM's success less likely. After 3 October, the White House decided that political factors rendered any option other than prompt withdrawal unattainable.

Working under UN direction proved a frustrating experience. Many senior US military officers came to look upon Jonathan Howe as the architect of disaster, determined to give UNOSOM a reach that far exceeded its grasp, and preoccupied with military solutions instead of political ones. That may be unfair, in that he was the energetic executor of a flawed policy. Obviously, in retrospect, the objectives prescribed by Resolution 814 were too ambitious. The US government usually played a central role in shaping policy but not always in executing it. "I realized after I got here what I was facing," Howe said in February 1994. "You can't have thirty different hands on the tiller."[2] So many of UNOSOM's contributors were either unresponsive or actually working at cross-purposes that the Force Commander found himself little more than a figurehead. The UN bureaucracy's shortcomings—under-manning, inertia, incompetence—compounded the difficulties and made failure almost inevitable. As an example, funds needed in June

1993 to subsidize militia demobilization and voluntary disarmament did not become available until January 1994.

The UN proved a suitable instrument for carrying out a humanitarian operation, but not a peace enforcement one. Joint Staff officers had started meeting regularly with UN counterparts in New York during December 1992 and recognized these shortcomings sooner than did many State Department and White House officials. Ultimately, though, disenchantment with UN peacekeeping was reflected in the stringent criteria that President Clinton applied on 3 May 1994 to any future US participation. According to PDD 25, the United States would either vote for or take the lead in calling for multilateral peace operations when, among other things: UN members were prepared to provide forces and funds; the US government judged political and military objectives to be clear and feasible; and UN involvement represented the best means of advancing US interests. Ordinarily, large-scale participation in peace enforcement that was likely to involve combat would be conducted either under US command or through competent regional organizations, such as NATO or ad hoc coalitions.[3] Seen from this perspective, the experience of the operation in Somalia seemed likely to cast a long shadow.

Acronyms

Notes

Chapter 1

[1] See John L. Hirsch and Robert B. Oakley, *Somalia and Operation Restore Hope* (1995), pp. 3-16.

[2] Memo, LtCol Van Esselstyn to Dir, J-3, "Somalia Working Group Meeting Notes," 30 Jul 92, C-OADR, J-3 JOD File, "Opn PROVIDE RELIEF, Memos," Bk 1; J-5 MEAF; "Conversational Topic: Humanitarian Support for Somalia," 31 Jul 92, J-5 MEAF File.

[3] Msg, Nairobi 243067 to SecState, 30 Jul 92, C-OADR, J-5 MEAF File. Not long afterward, Ambassador Hempstone paid a visit to Somalia. The State Department then instructed him not to visit the country again.

[4] Memo, Dir, J-4, to ASD(GA), "Request for Cost Estimates ...," 4 Aug 92, U, J-5 MEAF File.

[5] State Dept., "Recommendations on Somalia," 4 Aug 92, U; "Somalia Working Group Meeting Results, 5 Aug 92," C-OADR, J-3 JOD File, "Opn PROVIDE RELIEF, Memos," Bk. 1.

[6] Memo, LtCol Van Esselstyn to Dir, J-3, "Results of Somalia PCC," 12 Aug 92, S-OADR, J-3 JOD File, "Opn PROVIDE RELIEF, Memos," Bk. 1.

[7] J-5 MEAF Info Paper, "Military Operations Options ....," 14 Aug 92, U, J-5 MEAF File.

[8] J-5 MEAF Info Paper, "Deputies Committee Meeting on Somalia," 14 Aug 92, S-OADR, J-5 MEAF File.

[9] "Summary of Conclusions from NSC DC Meeting, 14 Aug 92," Att to Memo, Exec Secy NSC to SJS et al., 15 Aug 92, C-OADR, J-3 JOD File, "Opn PROVIDE RELIEF, Memos," Bk. 1; *Weekly Compilation of Presidential Documents: 1992*, pp. 1441-42. Natsios was Assistant Administrator for Food and Humanitarian Assistance, AID.

[10] Msg, CJCS to USCINCCENT, 151756Z Aug 92, C-OADR; Msg, USCINCCENT to Joint Staff, 152344Z Aug 92, C-OADR; Msg, CJCS to USCINCCENT, 170050Z Aug 92, C-OADR; J-3 JOD File, "Opn PROVIDE RELIEF, Msgs," Bk. 1. On 27 August, USCINCCENT decided to deploy two more C-130s and take away four C-141s. BGen Frank Libutti, USMC, became the Commander, Joint Task Force PROVIDE RELIEF.

[11] J-5 MEAF Info Paper, "Deputies Committee Meeting on Somalia," 20 Aug 92, C-OADR; "Summary of Conclusions for NSC Deputies Committee Meeting," 20 Aug 92, C-OADR, J-5 MEAF File.

[12] Memo, COL Brittain to Dir, J-3, "Somalia PCC," 1 Sep 92, U, J-3 JOD File, "Opn PRO-VIDE RELIEF, Memos," Bk. 1; "Summary of PCC Meeting on Somalia," Att to Memo, Exec Secy NSC to SJS et al., 3 Sep 92, C-OADR, J-5 MEAF File; J-5 MEAF Info Paper, "DC Meeting on Somalia," 28 Sep 92, C-OADR, J-3 JOD File, "Opn PROVIDE RELIEF, Memos," Bk. 3.

[13] Info Paper by Somalia Working Group, "Current and Near-Term Situation in Somalia," 22 Sep 92, S-OADR, J-3 JOD File, "Opn PROVIDE RELIEF, Memos," Bk. 3. The long-neglected asphalt runway at Baidoa soon began to deteriorate.

[14] Tab D in J-5 MEAF Binder "DC Mtg on Somalia," 4 Sep 92.

[15] "Summary of PCC Meeting on Somalia," Att to Memo, Exec Secy NSC to SJS et al., 24 Sep 92, C-OADR, J-5 MEAF File. J-5 MEAF Info Paper, "DC Meeting on Somalia," 28 Sep 92, C-OADR, J-3 JOD File, "Opn PROVIDE RELIEF, Memos," Bk. 3.

[16] TelCon, ADM David Jeremiah, USN (Ret.), with W. S. Poole, 10 Oct 94; MFR by Paul Kinsinger, "Deputies Committee Meeting on Somalia, 28 September," 29 Sep 92, S-OADR, J-3 JOD File, "Opn PROVIDE RELIEF, Memos," Bk 3. Lieutenant Colonel Wahlquist believed that ADM Jeremiah's stops in Kenya and Somalia on 23-24 September had led the Vice Chairman to change his view about the feasibility of shifting rapidly from a primar-ily military airlift to a civilian one. Jeremiah, through his Executive Assistant, informed RADM Bowman that transition planning should be driven by events and not by calendar deadlines. Reducing or eliminating DoD's airlift role, ADM Jeremiah now felt, was accept-able only (1) if such action did not reduce the total delivery of relief supplies and (2) if the Somali clans made progress toward political reconciliation. At Bowman's suggestion, Wahlquist redrafted the 28 Sep Information Paper to capture these views. In effect, the Joint Staff was moving closer to State's position.

[17] Msg, Nairobi 1658 to SecState, 1 Oct 92, C-OADR, Tab to "PCC Mtg on Somalia, 9 Oct 92"; J-5 MEAF Info Paper, "'Points of Security': Case Study in Baidoa," 9 Oct 92, S-OADR; MFR, LTC Baltimore to Col Berger, "PCC on Somalia, 9 Oct 92," 9 Oct 92, S-OADR, J-5 MEAF Binder for "PCC Mtg on Somalia, 9 Oct 92," J-5 MEAF File; "Summary of PCC Mtg on Somalia," Att to Memo, Exec Secy NSC to SJS et al., n.d., C-OADR; "Interagency Planning Group Status Report," 15 Oct 92, S-OADR, J-3 JOD File, "Opn PROVIDE RELIEF, Memos," Bk. 4.

[18] "Summary of Conclusions of Deputies Committee Meeting on Somalia," 21 Oct 92, C-OADR; J-5 MEAF Info Paper, "PCC Mtg on Somalia," 29 Oct 92, C-OADR, J-5 MEAF File. By 1 November, US military aircraft had flown 942 sorties and delivered 11,165 met-ric tons of relief supplies.

[19] J-5 MEAF Info Paper, n.d., C-OADR, J-5 MEAF File.

[20] J-5 MEAF Form 136, "UN Request for Additional Airlift to Somalia," 5 Nov 92, C-OADR, J-5 MEAF File; Memo, ASD(ISA) to SecDef and DepSecDef, same subj. and date, C-OADR, J-3 JOD File, "Opn PROVIDE RELIEF, Memos," Bk. 5.

Chapter 2

[1] "Summary of PCC Meeting on Somalia," Att to Memo, Exec Secy NSC to SJS et al., 10 Nov 92, C-OADR; DCI, National Intelligence Council Memo, "Can United Nations Force Successfully Carry Out Their Mission in Somalia?" 10 Nov 92, S-OADR, J-5 MEAF Master File; Info Paper by LTC Bray, J-3 JOD, "Points of Security: Bardera Case Study," C-OADR, J-4 LRC Files, "Somalia Relief" Folder.

[2] Msg, USUN 5143 to SecState, 6 Nov 92, S, J-3 JOD File, "Opn Provide Relief, Memos," Bk. 5. COL Perry Baltimore, USA, interviewed by W. S. Poole 28 Apr 95.

[3] Memo, COL Brittain to Chief, J-3 JOD, "Request for USCINCCENT Assessment of USUN Message," 12 Nov 92, C, J-3 JOD File, "Opn Provide Relief, Memos," Bk. 5.

[4] "Summary of PCC Meeting on Somalia," C-OADR, Tab A-1 in J-5 MEAF Binder for DC Mtg on Somalia, 20 Nov 92; J-5 MEAF Info Paper, "PCC Meeting on Somalia," 12 Nov 92, S-OADR; Ltr, UNSYG to Pres UNSC, 24 Nov 92, U, J-5 MEAF File.

[5] Msg, USUN 5420 to SecState, 17 Nov 92, C-OADR, J-4 LRC Files, "PROVIDE RELIEF: Sit Reps/Msgs, 10 Nov-31 Dec 92."

[6] Msg, USUN 5526 to SecState, 21 Nov 92, C-OADR, J-5 MEAF File.

[7] J-5 MEAF Info/TP, "Small Group Meeting on Somalia," 23 Nov 92, S-OADR, J-3 JOD File, "Opn Provide Relief, Memos," Bk. 6; "USCINCCENT Commander's Estimate," 22 Nov 92, S, J-5 MEAF File.

[8] Msg, Nairobi 25912 to SecState, 20 Nov 92, C-OADR, J-5 MEAF File.

[9] Discussion Paper, "Somalia Security Options," 20 Nov 92, S, J-5 MEAF File.

[10] "Spectrum of US Role Across Three Options," 22 Nov 92, S, J-5 MEAF File. The cost of Option 1 was estimated at $250 million in FY 1993. Option 2 would require an additional $250 million—or, if other countries did not contribute, $1 billion. Assuming that the United States furnished most of the troops, Option 3 would cost between $850 million and $1.25 billion more than Option 1. "Rough Estimate of Costs to the US of Somalia Options," 23 Nov 92, S-OADR, J-5 MEAF File.

[11] J-5 MEAF Info/TP for VCJCS, "Small Group Deputies Committee Meeting on Somalia," 24 Nov 92, S-OADR, J-5 MEAF File.

[12] GEN Colin L. Powell interviewed by BG D. A. Armstrong, USA(Ret.) and W. S. Poole, 21 Feb 95. Before the NSC meeting, all participants were given a paper that described the three options cited above. Memo, Exec Secy NSC to CJCS et al., "Presidential Meeting on Somalia, November 25 at 9:00 AM," 24 Nov 92, S-OADR, J-5 MEAF File. The Chairman also received the Wahlquist-Baltimore draft; the J-5 MEAF Info/TP, "NSC Principals Meeting on Somalia," 25 Nov 92, S-OADR, bears the stamp, "CJCS has seen." In the 1995 interview, GEN Powell could not recall whether he presented all three options at the meeting. Joint Staff officers were not told what advice GEN Powell had presented.

[13] ADM Jeremiah telcon with W. S. Poole, 10 Oct 94. A *Washington Post* story on 6 December claimed that ADM Jeremiah said: "if you think U.S. forces are needed...we can do the job" during a DC meeting on 21 November. Actually, the Assistant to the Chairman, LTG

Barry R. McCaffrey, attended that meeting. ADM Jeremiah went to meetings on 23 and 24 November, and spoke the words quoted at one of those sessions. TelCon, ADM Jeremiah with COL Perry Baltimore, 10 Dec 93, and related by COL Baltimore to W. S. Poole.

[14] That remained GEN McCaffrey's position throughout the US involvement. MFR by BG David Armstrong, USA (Ret.), "PHONECON with GEN Barry McCaffrey," 5 Oct 95.

[15] GEN Colin L. Powell interviewed by BG D. A. Armstrong, USA (Ret.) and W. S. Poole, 21 Feb 95. USS *Tripoli* and USS *Guam* were LPHs displacing 18,800 tons.

[16] Msg, SecState 387178 to USUN, 1 Dec 92, S-OADR; J-5 MEAF TP/Info Paper, "Small Group Teleconference on Somalia," 1 Dec 92, S-OADR; J-5 MEAF File; Msg, CJCS to USCINCCENT, 011335Z Dec 92, S-OADR, J-3 JOD File, "Opn Restore Hope, Memos," Bk. 1.

[17] J-5 MEAF Info/TP, "DC Meeting on Somalia," 2 Dec 92, J-5 MEAF File.

[18] Dept of State, *Dispatch*, 14 Dec 92, pp. 883-884. This resolution marked the first time that the UN acted under Chapter VII of the UN Charter without having been invited to intervene.

[19] Ltr, President Bush to UNSYG, 4 Dec 92, J-5 MEAF File.

[20] Msg, CJCS to USCINCCENT, 021925Z Dec 92, S-OADR, J-3 JOD File, "Operation Restore Hope, Memos," Bk. 1. Msg, Joint Staff J-3 to USCINCCENT, 062030Z Dec 92, S-OADR; J-5 MEAF Info/TP, "Small Group DC Teleconference on Somalia," 7 Dec 92, S-OADR; Ltr, UNSYG to Pres Bush, 8 Dec 92, J-5 MEAF File.

[21] Meade and Chilcoat were serving in the Army's Office of the Deputy Chief of Staff, Plans and Operations. Another factor—although evidently not the decisive one—that entered into Army calculations was a worry that the 10th Mountain Division could be slated for deactivation during the next round of downsizing. Very recently, some of its units had been sent to Florida in the wake of Hurricane Andrew to assist with disaster relief. Participating in Operation RESTORE HOPE could enhance the Division's image. LtCol Ritchie M. Lilly, USMC, 6 Apr 93; LTC Robert M. Bray, USA, 7 May 93; and COL Frank W. Brittain, USA, 7 May 93, all members of J-3 JOD, interviewed by W. S. Poole.

[22] Msg, USCINCCENT to Joint Staff, 040015Z Dec 92, S-OADR; Msg, CJCS to USCINC-CENT, 051823Z Dec 92, S-OADR, J-3 JOD File, Tab 1A in "Restore Hope, Memos," Bk. 1.

[23] Msg, USCINCCENT to Joint Staff, J-5, 020330Z Dec 92, S-OADR; Msg, USCINC-TRANS to USCENTCOM, 070216Z Dec 92; J-4 LRC File, "Restore Hope: Sit Reps/Msgs, 4-8 Dec 92."

[24] SOA 69, "Flow of ARFOR Forces into Somalia," 26 Dec 92, S-OADR, J-4 LRC File, "Restore Hope: Status of Actions 1-112."

[25] Msg, USCINCTRANS to USCENTCOM, 160257Z Dec 92, S-OADR, J-4 LRC File, "RESTORE HOPE: Sit Reps/Msgs, 15-19 Dec 92." The same problem of having to rely upon an ad hoc system had arisen in 1990 during DESERT SHIELD deployments to the Persian Gulf. Information in the remainder of this paragraph comes from a J-4 Briefing to the Joint Staff in Apr 93.

[26] Msg, SecState 394279 to CJTF PROVIDE RELIEF, 8 Dec 92, C-OADR, J-5 MEAF File.

[27] Draft Msg, USUN to SecState, 9 Dec 92, C-OADR, J-5 MEAF File.

[28] UNOSOM I consisted of the five hundred Pakistanis at Mogadishu airport plus the four battalions that had not yet deployed.

[29] "Summary of Conclusions for Core Group Meeting on Somalia, December 10, 1992, 10:00 AM," S; "Summary of Conclusions of Deputies Committee Meeting on Somalia," 11 Dec 92, Att to Memo, Exec Secy NSC to SJS et al., 12 Dec 92, S, J-5 MEAF File.

[30] J-5 MEAF Info Paper, "Options for US Role in UNOSOM II," n.d., S-OADR, J-5 MEAF File.

[31] J-5 MEAF Info Paper, "NSC Core Group Meeting on Somalia," 16 Dec 92, S-OADR, J-5 MEAF File.

[32] Msg, SecState 409375 to Lagos et al., 20 Dec 92, S-OADR, J-5 MEAF File.

[33] J-5 MEAF Info Paper, "NSC DC Group Meeting on Somalia," 23 Dec 92, S-OADR, J-5 MEAF File.

[34] J-5 MEAF Info Paper, "Proposed US Role in UNOSOM II in Somalia," 23 Dec 92, S-OADR, J-5 MEAF File.

[35] Msg, SecState 591 to Rome et al., 4 Jan 93, S-OADR; Msg, Geneva 11231 to SecState, 30 Dec 92, C-OADR, J-5 MEAF File.

[36] MFR by RADM Bowman, "6 Jan 93 UN Meeting on Somalia," 7 Jan 93, C-OADR, J-5 MEAF File.

[37] J-5 MEAF Info Paper, "NSC Core Group Teleconference on Somalia," 4 Jan 93, S-OADR, J-5 MEAF File. None of these contributors was entirely self-sufficient.

[38] J-5 MEAF Info Paper, "NSC Core Group Teleconference on Somalia," [ca 4 Feb 93] J-5 MEAF File. The amendment's author was Sen. Larry Pressler (R, SD). J-5 MEAF Info Paper, "NSC Core Group Meeting on Somalia," 16 Dec 92, S-OADR; Msg, Islamabad 18292 to SecState, 14 Dec 92, C-OADR; J-5A 6593-93 to DJS, 18 Dec 92, S-OADR, J-5 MEAF File.

[39] J-5 MEAF Info Paper, ca 4 Feb 93, cited above; Msg, SecState 52971 to Islamabad, 21 Feb 93, C-OADR, J-3 JOD File, "Opn Restore Hope, UNOSOM II, Kuwait-Zimbabwe." The Trust Fund then contained $115 million, mostly contributed by Japan. It was intended to defray transportation and in-country expenses of troops contributed by poorer nations.

[40] J-5 MEAF Info Paper, "Somali Police and Guard Force Issues," 13 Jan 93, S-OADR; Msg, SecState 491 to USLO Mogadishu, 2 Jan 93, S-OADR, J-5 MEAF File.

[41] Msg, Mogadishu 75 to SecState, 12 Jan 93, C-OADR; J-5 MEAF Info Paper, "Somali Police and Guard Force Issues," 13 Jan 93; Draft Msg, SecState to Mogadishu, 5 Feb 93, C, J-5 MEAF File.

[42] Msg, USLO Mogadishu 45 to SecState, 8 Jan 93; Msg, Mogadishu 76 to SecState, 12 Jan 93, J-5 MEAF File.

[43] Rpt, Cmdr, UNITAF to USCENTCOM, J-3 & Dir, J-5, Joint Staff, "Commander's Assessment of Operation RESTORE HOPE," 28 Jan 93, U, J-5 MEAF File.

[44] Ltr, SecDef to Dir, OMB, 12 Jan 93, U, J-4 LRC File, "RESTORE HOPE: Sit Reps/Msgs, 8-13 Jan 93." By late March, the estimate of US costs during FY 1993 had risen to $1.2 billion, with the Defense Department paying $852 million.

[45] GAO Rpt to Congressional Committees, "Peace Operations: Cost of DOD Operations in Somalia," Mar 94, U.

[46] The State Department's latest draft avoided mentioning either the UN Charter's Chapter VI ("peaceful settlement of disputes") or Chapter VII ("enforcement") in order to preserve flexibility. The draft would authorize UNOSOM II to "ensure the maintenance of a secure environment for humanitarian relief operations, taking all appropriate actions against elements threatening that secure environment, and to promote reconciliation and a political settlement in Somalia." As will be seen, that came fairly close to the language finally adopted. Draft Text of UNSC Resolution, n.d. [ca 25 Jan 93], J-5 MEAF File.

[47] J-5 MEAF Info Paper, "NSC Deputies Committee Meeting on Somalia," 25 Jan 93, S-OADR; "Planning Assumptions for US Military Presence in Somalia," n.d., S-OADR, J-5 MEAF File.

[48] J-5 MEAF File.

[49] Memo, USD(P) to SecDef, "Somalia: The January 28 Principals Meeting," 27 Jan 93, S-OADR, J-5 MEAF File.

[50] Msg, USCINCCENT to Joint Staff, 292250Z Jan 93, C-OADR; Ltr, USCINCCENT to CJCS, 27 Jan 93, U, J-5 MEAF File. This withdrawal plan already had gone through revisions and would undergo more.

[51] J-5 MEAF Information Paper, "US Logistics Support for UNOSOM II," 7 Apr 93, S-OADR, J-5 MEAF File. In preparation for the 28 Jan meeting, GEN Powell read J-5 MEAF Talking Paper, "NSC PC Mtg on Somalia," 28 Jan 93, S-OADR, J-5 MEAF File. It contained the views about UNOSOM II and the QRF that are outlined above. Msg, USLO Mogadishu to USCINCCENT et al., 311313Z Jan 93, C-OADR, J-5 MEAF File.

[52] Memo, DATP(NSA) to VCJCS et al., "Somalia Core Group-Taskings," 8 Feb 93, S-OADR.

[53] Memo, Exec Secy, State Dept. to Exec Secy, NSC, "Conclusions Reached at the February 26 Interagency Working Group Meeting on Somalia," 5 Mar 93, S-OADR; National Intelligence Council Memorandum, "Somalia: Searching for a Political Solution—the Next 24 Months," 22 Feb 93, S; J-5 MEAF File.

[54] Howe had difficulty recruiting US personnel for his staff. He asked DoD for an officer who would serve as liaison with MG Montgomery, but no one was ever assigned. LTC Michael A. Sheehan, USA, interviewed by W. S. Poole, 20 Jul 95. The State Department also had difficulty in finding personnel to serve in Somalia.

[55] J-5 MEAF Info Paper, "US Logistics Support for UNOSOM II," 7 Apr 93, S-OADR, J-5 MEAF File. LtGen Johnston, one month later, informed General Powell that twenty-six

hundred logistic troops would be needed in UNITAF's area of operations. Contractors were meeting other requirements.

[56] MG Waldo Freeman, USA, interviewed by BG Armstrong and W. S. Poole, 17 July 2000. LTG McCaffrey, who was now Director, J-5, later recalled having pressed for a more powerful QRF: either a battalion task force with M1A1 tanks and Bradley fighting vehicles or an armored cavalry unit, as well as Apache attack helicopters. GEN Powell followed the normal practice of relying upon the unified commander to determine the composition of the force. MFR by BG Armstrong, "Phonecon with GEN Barry McCaffrey," 5 Oct 95.

[57] PDD/NSC-6, "US Policy on Somalia," 19 May 93, Att to SM-124-93 to CJCS et al., 24 May 93, S. Two portions of PDD-6 took the Joint Staff by surprise: first, the QRF's departure being made a matter for President Clinton's decision; second, major redeployments being made a matter for approval by the Deputies Committee. COL Perry Baltimore, USA, J-5 MEAF, interviewed by W. S. Poole, 24 May 93. The QRF consisted of the 1st Battalion, 22d Infantry Regiment; the 3d Battalion, 25th Aviation Regiment; the 10th Forward Support Battalion (all from the 10th Mountain Division); and a Special Operations Command Element. Eight Cobra helicopter gunships stayed with the QRF.

[58] Msg, USLO Mogadishu 151 to SecState, 24 Jan 93, C. ADM David Jeremiah, USN (Ret.), interviewed by Dr. Lorna Jaffe, 16 Jun 94. ADM Jeremiah telcon with W. S. Poole, 10 Oct 94.

Chapter 3

[1] According to MG Freeman, USCENTCOM saw the cantonment of weapons as a way to promote disarming without challenging the Somalis' manhood. Howe broke the agreement between UNITAF and clan leaders by insisting upon inventory followed by confiscation. MG Freeman interviewed by BG Armstrong and W. S. Poole, 17 July 2000.

[2] MAJ Fred T. Pribble, USA, and Col James P. Terry, USMC, Chairman's Legal Counsel, interviewed by W. S. Poole, 25 May 95. Telcon, VADM Frank P. Bowman with W. S. Poole, 31 Aug 95. GEN Colin L. Powell, USA (Ret.), interviewed by BG David Armstrong, USA (Ret.), and W. S. Poole, 21 Feb 95. Mr. Lake later claimed that GEN Powell had approved the draft before it was sent to New York, but when Powell challenged that claim the NSC Staff specified only a telephone conversation with an unidentified Joint Staff officer.

[3] Msg, USCINCCENT to Joint Staff, 062345Z Jun 93, S; Ltr, Jonathan Howe to USYG Annan, 8 Jun 93, C, J-5 MEAF File. Howe did not provide a concept of operations.

[4] Memo, USCENTCOM J-3 to Joint Staff J-3, "U.S. Logistics Support for UNOSOM II," 21 Jul 93, S, J-3 JOD File, "UNOSOM II, Current Issues, Vol. III." On 7 Jun, MG Montgomery sent USYG Annan an urgent request for fifteen items of riot and crowd control equipment. The UN asked the United States to supply six items. Five were sent; shipment of CS gas [tear gas] was delayed for legal review.

[5] Msg, SecState 176657 to USUN, 11 Jun 93, C, J-5 MEAF File; Memo, DCI Rep to JCS to CJCS et al., "COS Mogadishu Ops Report," 9 Jun 93, S, J-3 JOD File, "UNOSOM II, Current Issues, Vol. I."

[6] FRAGO No. 43 by LTG Bir, 15 Jun 93, S; Msg, SecState 182748 to CJCS, 16 Jun 93, S, J-5 MEAF File; "USFORSOM After Action Report" by LTG Montgomery, Jun 94. Great

care was taken to limit Somali casualties. Warnings were broadcast 15, 10 and 5 minutes beforehand; helicopter searchlights pinpointed the building that was targeted; and then 20 mm. rounds were fired at the roof. MG Montgomery always submitted concept plans to USCINCCENT; the plans then went to Defense and State for review. LTG Thomas M. Montgomery, USA, interviewed by W. S. Poole, 21 Jun 95.

[7] Information Paper by COL Baltimore for DC Mtg on Somalia, 15 Jun 93, S; Washfax, State to J-5 et al., 21 Jun 93, C; J-5A 3205-95 to DJS, 22 Jun 93, C; Def Int Rpt, J-2 383-93, "Somalia: Situation Update," 24 Jun 93, S; J-5 MEAF File CT. Soon afterward, COL Baltimore became MEAF Division Chief; Col Jeffrey A. Wall, USAF, succeeded him as Africa Branch Chief.

[8] Memo, "Somalia: Dealing with Aideed," 12 Jul 93, S, J-5 MEAF File; Msg, 140139Z Jul 93, C, J-3 JOD File, "UNOSOM II, Current Issues, Vol. III." LTG Montgomery interviewed by W. S. Poole, 21 Jun 95. Several times, before 17 June, US helicopters had tracked Aideed and hovered above him. Telcon, ADM Jonathan Howe, USN (Ret), with W. S. Poole, 3 Oct 95. Howe recalled that the idea of a reward originated with UNOSOM officers, mainly Americans, who argued that otherwise Somalis would not treat the arrest warrant seriously. Howe tried and failed to get US funds, then turned to UN headquarters. The SNA, meantime, was putting larger bounties upon the heads of Somalis who worked for UNOSOM.

[9] LTC Michael A. Sheehan, USA, interviewed by W. S. Poole, 20 Jul 95. Montgomery made this statement on 3 July 1993. Next day, from Bangkok, LTC Sheehan sent the State Department a cable conveying this information.

[10] MG Waldo Freeman, USA (Ret), interviewed by BG Armstrong and W. S. Poole, 17 July 2000. MG Patrick L. Hughes, USA, who in 1993 was USCENTCOM J-2, later recalled that General Hoar's 1-in-4 estimate originated at a June meeting of USCINCCENT with his J-2 and J-3. Hughes visited Mogadishu in July believing that Aideed could be captured. But then he went with a SEAL team into the heart of the city and met a "source" who had been a police chief under Siad Barre. An officer with considerable experience, Hughes felt that he had never encountered a man who was more brutal—and there were many Somalis like him. Hughes then decided that the odds of success were indeed only 1-in-4 and recommended against sending SOF. MG Hughes interviewed by BG Armstrong and W. S. Poole, 17 Oct 95; Telcon, ADM Howe with W. S. Poole, 3 Oct 95.

[11] Draft Memo, ASD(ISA) to SecDef, "Dealing with Aideed," 28 Jun 93, S-OADR, J-3 JOD File, "UNOSOM II, Current Issues, Vol. II"; *Washington Post*, 3 Apr 94, p. 12; Msg, USLO Mogadishu 1556 to SecState, 9 Jul 93, C; J-5 Form 136, "Options for Dealing with Aideed," 15 Jul 93, S-OADR; J-5, "Somalia Options Paper," 17 Jul 93, S; Memo, LtCol Lilly to Chief, WHEM, J-3, "Somalia Game Plan and Options," 22 Jul 93, U; Memo, Dir, J-5 to CJCS, 26 Jul 93, S; J-3 JOD File, "UNOSOM II, Current Issues, Vol. III." Col Wahlquist's Notebook, 20 Jul 93; ADM David Jeremiah, USN (Ret), interviewed by Dr. Lorna Jaffe, 16 Jun 94; GEN Colin L. Powell, USA (Ret), interviewed by BG David Armstrong, USA (Ret) and W. S. Poole, 21 Feb 95.

[12] The team's final report is in Msg, USLO Mogadishu to SecState, 271112Z Jul 93, S, J-5 MEAF File. See also Talking Points by COL Baltimore, "Somalia Round Table Discussion with SecDef," 3 & 10 Aug 93, S, J-5 MEAF File.

[13] GEN Colin L. Powell, USA (Ret), interviewed by BG David Armstrong, USA (Ret) and W. S. Poole, 21 Feb 95. The team, however, had come at Howe's request. MG Freeman believed that its purpose, from the outset, was to justify sending SOF. MG Freeman Interview.

[14] "Summary of Conclusions of Meeting of the NSC Deputies Committee" on 4 Aug 93, Att to Memo, Exec Secy, NSC to SJS et al., 10 Aug 93, S, J-3 JOD File, "UNOSOM II, Current Issues, Vol. IV."

[15] "Summary of Conclusions of Meeting of the NSC Deputies Committee," 16 Aug 93, S-OADR, J-5 MEAF File. Admirals Jeremiah and Bowman attended the meeting.

[16] Memo, Dir, J-5, to VCJCS, "Plus-up for Egyptian Participation in UNOSOM II," 17 Aug 93, U; J-5A 04308-93 to VCJCS, 19 Aug 93, S-OADR; Msg, USDAO Cairo to Joint Staff, 241555Z Aug 93, J-5 MEAF File; Msg, Pres Clinton to Pres Mubarak, 151719Z Sep 93, S, J-5 MEAF File.

[17] GEN Powell Interview.

[18] GEN Powell Interview; *Washington Post*, 3 Apr 94, pp. 10, 12 and 30 Jan 94, p. 13. Three force packages for Task Force Ranger were presented, each of which included AC-130s. The Commander in Chief, Special Operations Command, GEN Wayne A. Downing, USA, wanted AC-130s but believed that Task Force Ranger could perform its mission without them and did not press the matter. General Hoar judged AC-130s unnecessary, chiefly because of his concern over the collateral damage they could inflict. The Joint Staff also recommended against including AC-130s in the force package. Senate Armed Services Committee, "Review of ... the Ranger Raid," pp. 28-31. GEN Powell, in an interview with BG Armstrong and W. S. Poole on 21 May 1996, said that he had no recollection of the AC-130 issue being brought to him. The Senate Report stated, without evidence, that he "evidently" recommended against including AC-130s.

[19] Msg, USCINCCENT to CJCS, 202031Z Aug 93, S-OADR, J-5 MEAF File.

[20] *New York Times*, 28 Aug 93, pp. 1, 4.

[21] "Summary of Conclusions of the Somalia Working Group's Teleconference on September 2, 1993," U; Talking Points by LTC Colvin, "J-4 Comments on Concept for Somalia National Police Force," 1 Sep 93, U; Presidential Determination No. 93-43 to SecDef and SecState, 30 Sep 93, J-5 MEAF File.

[22] "Detailed Rpt on 5 Sep 93 Incident at Checkpoint 42 in North Mogadishu," 7 Sep 93 by LTC Oyinlola, U, Col Wahlquist File.

[23] Msg, SecState 272687 to USLO Mogadishu, 5 Sep 93, S; Msg, USLO Mogadishu 1920 to SecState, 6 Sep 93, S-OADR; Msgs, USCINCCENT to CJCS, 061735Z and 062030 Sep 93, S-OADR; Msg, USCINCCENT to CJCS, 081632Z Sep 93, S, J-3 JOD File "Current Issues, UNOSOM II, Vol. V"; Senate Armed Services Committee Report, "Review of ... the Ranger Raid," pp. 29-30. By this time senior American military officers did not hold Ambassador Gosende in high regard.

[24] Memo, USD(P) to CJCS, 8 Sep 93, Att to Draft Memo, USD(P) to SecDef, "Somalia: Exploring a Political Settlement," 8 Sep 93, S-OADR, J-3 JOD File, "UNOSOM II, Current Issues, Vol. II." Evidently this draft never went to the Secretary of Defense.

[25] USFORSOM After Action Report by MG Montgomery, Jun 94; ADM Jeremiah Interview.

[26] Memo, Exec Secy, NSC to SJS et al., "Summary of Conclusions of Deputies Committee Meeting on Somalia, September 11, 1993," 13 Sep 93, S-OADR, J-5 MEAF File; Draft Memo, USD(P) to SecDef, "Toward a Strategy for Somalia," 11 Sep 93, C, J-3 JOD File, "UNOSOM II, Current Issues, Vol. VI." The career UN staff in Mogadishu pursued a top-down approach of working with warlords to organize a power-sharing confederation. USFORSOM After Action Report by MG Montgomery, Jun 94, S.

[27] Col Wahlquist's Notebook, 9 Sep 93. Hoar also told Gosende that he felt the USLO was intruding into operational matters.

[28] Letter, Ambassador Gosende to AsstSecState George Moose, 15 Sep 93, C. Subsequently, the USCENTCOM Chief of Staff told Gosende that limitations were imposed by Washington, not Tampa. Msg, USLO Mogadishu 2135 to SecState, 29 Sep 93, S.

[29] Draft Memo, OASD(RSA) to USD(P) and SecDef, "Somalia Exit Strategy," 16 Sep 93, S-OADR; Memo, Dir, J-5, to CJCS, 17 Sep 93, U, J-3 JOD File, "UNOSOM II, Current Issues, Vol. VI."

[30] Msg, USLO 2055 Mogadishu to SecState, 18 Sep 93, C; *Washington Post*, 11 Nov 93, p. 39.

[31] State Dept., "Draft Non-Paper: Somalia: Where Do We Go From Here?" n.d. (20 Sep 93)," S; Memo by Vice Dir, J-2 (COL J. W. Pardew, USA), "Somalia," 30 Sep 93, S; Ltr, UNSYG to SecState, 25 Sep 93, U, J-5 MEAF File. GEN Powell did not know about the State Department's 20 September paper. US Senate Armed Services Committee Report, "Review of Ranger ... Raid," p. 44.

[32] Msg, USLO Mogadishu 2092 to SecState, 24 Sep 93, C; Msg, USLO Mogadishu 2135 to SecState, 29 Sep 93, S; Memo, USCINCCENT to GEN Powell, "Some Thoughts on Somalia," 27 Sep 93, S, J-3 JOD File, "UNOSOM II, Current Issues, Vol. VI."

[33] Msg, SecState 291176 to USLO Mogadishu, 23 Sep 93, C.

[34] Memo, Dir, J-5, to CJCS, "US Forces Withdrawal Plan from Somalia," 28 Sep 93, S, J-5 MEAF File; *NY Times*, 30 Sep 93, p. 1.

[35] US Senate Committee on Armed Services Rpt, "Review of Ranger Raid," pp. 35, 44.

[36] *NY Times*, 28 Sep 93, p. 1.

[37] GEN Colin L. Powell, USA (Ret) interviewed by BG David A. Armstrong, USA (Ret) and W. S. Poole 21 May 1996; ADM Jeremiah Interview, 16 Jun 94.

[38] Telcon Mr. Clark Murdock with W. S. Poole, 27 & 28 Apr 95.

[39] Telcon, VADM Frank P. Bowman with W. S. Poole, 31 Aug 95.

[40] Telcon, ADM Howe with W. S. Poole, 3 Oct 95. When MG Garrison read this passage, he commented that Howe "was not told by any members of Task Force Ranger that we were optimistic about getting Aideed." Letter, USSOCOM Historian to JHO, 12 Feb 96. According to MG Hughes and MG Freeman, senior officers of Task Force Ranger contin-

ued displaying a "can-do" attitude, while higher levels in both Special Operations Command and USCENTCOM rated Aideed's capture as possible but not necessarily probable. MG Hughes, 17 Oct 95, and MG Freeman, 17 Jul 2000, interviewed by BG David Armstrong and W. S. Poole.

[41] Msg, COMUSFORSOMALIA to USCINCCENT, 141900Z Sep 93, S; Memo, USCINCCENT to CJCS, "Additional Forces," 22 Sep 93, S, J-3 JOD File, "UNOSOM II, Current Issues, Vol. VI"; USFORSOM After Action Report by MG Montgomery, Jun 94, S; US Senate Armed Services Committee Report, "Review of the ... Ranger Raid," pp. 25, 34. In LTG McCaffrey's view, USCINCCENT had earlier constituted the primary opposition to placing armor in Mogadishu. BG Armstrong, MFR, "PHONECON with GEN Barry McCaffrey," 5 Oct 95; *Washington Post*, 31 Oct 93, pp. 1, 5; GEN Powell Interview, 21 Feb 95.

[42] A vivid account of the battle is given in Mark Bowden, *Black Hawk Down* (NY, Atlantic Monthly Press, 1999). In his memoir, President Clinton states that "when I approved the use of U. S. forces to apprehend Aideed, I did not envision anything like a daytime assault in a crowded, hostile neighborhood. I assumed we would try to get him when he was on the move.... Apparently, that's also what Colin Powell thought he was asking me to approve; when I discussed it with him after I left the White House..., Powell said he would not have approved an operation like that unless it was conducted at night. But we hadn't discussed that, nor apparently had anyone else imposed any parameters on General Garrison's range of options." William J. Clinton, *My Life* (NY: Alfred A. Knopf, 2004), pp. 552-553.

[43] ADM Jeremiah Interview, 16 Jun 94, U; "Completing the U.S. Mission in Somalia," Att to Memo, Dir, J-5, to RADM Luecke, 3 Oct 93, S.

[44] Telcon, Mr. Clark Murdock with W. S. Poole, 28 Apr 95.

[45] COL Perry Baltimore, USA, interviewed by W. S. Poole, 28 Apr 95.

[46] Testimony of Gen Joseph Hoar before the Senate Armed Services Committee, 13 Oct 93, and of MG Thomas Montgomery and MG William Garrison, 12 May 94, U.

[47] The Attorney General, at one point, indicated a belief that the fighting on 3 October constituted "hostilities" as defined by Section 5B of the War Powers Resolution. Earlier, the administration had reviewed issues associated with the Resolution and decided to institute periodic consultations with senior members of Congress. The Chairman's Legal Counsel, Col James P. Terry, USMC, gave his opinion that the confrontation with Aideed was international police action analogous to the eradication of an international terrorist organization, a circumstance never held to equate to hostilities. Although this issue remained unresolved, the Legal Counsel's position did attract a good deal of interagency support. Information Paper by Col Terry, "War Powers Issues—PRD 28," 2 Sep 93, C; "Summary of Conclusions of Principals Committee Meeting on War Powers Issues," 2 Sep 93, Att to Memo, Exec Secy, NSC to SJS et al., 7 Sep 93, S; Memo, Col J. P. Terry, USMC, to DoD and CIA General Counsels, "Application of Section 5B of the War Powers Resolution to the Current Situation in Somalia," 12 Oct 93, U.

[48] MFR, "Phonecon with GEN Barry McCaffrey," 5 Oct 95. The storage sites proved to be empty.

[49] J-3 JOD Issue Paper, "U.S. Deployment Timelines," 5 Oct 93, S; J-3, "Projected Force Options in Mogadishu," n.d., S, J-3 JOD File. Telcons, LtCol Ritchie Lilly, USMC, 3 Oct 94 and ADM David Jeremiah, 10 Oct 94 with W. S. Poole. In fact, a movement of one Marine Amphibious Ready Group had been planned. *Weekly Compilation of Presidential Documents, 1993*, pp. 2023-2025. To implement new policies, Richard Clarke of the NSC Staff and James Dobbins of the State Department co-chaired a Somalia Coordination Committee that reported to the Deputies Committee.

[50] Memo, Dir, J-5, to VCJCS, "Non-Paper: Completing the U. S. Military Mission in Somalia," 8 Oct 93, U, Folder, "UNOSOM II, Current Issues," Vol. VII, J-3 JOD File.

[51] LTC Gordon Kennedy, USA, interviewed by W. S. Poole 14 Oct 94; "Logistics Transition Update," 5 Nov 93, U; "Executive Logistic Talking Points, Executive Committee Meeting, 5 Nov 93," J-5 MEAF File; "Logistics Transition Update," 6 Nov 93, S-OADR, J-5 MEAF File"; J-5 Issue Paper, "Somalia Update," 2 Dec 93, S-OADR, J-5 MEAF File. Brown and Root used two hundred US civilians, mostly retired military personnel, and about two thousand Somalis.

[52] Msg, USCINCCENT to COMUSFORSOMALIA, 152300Z Oct 93, S, J-5 MEAF File; MG Carl F. Ernst, USA, 17 Jan 95 and LTG Thomas M. Montgomery, USA, 21 Jun 95 interviewed by W. S. Poole. Montgomery originally suggested that he be Commander, JTF Somalia, but USCINCCENT decided that would give him too many responsibilities.

[53] "USCINCCENT Strategic Concept for the Redeployment of Forces from Somalia," 9 Nov 93, S, OPORD/USFORSCOM 2, 280758Z Nov 93, J-5 MEAF File; Msg, USLO Mogadishu 2364 to SecState, 29 Oct 93, C.

[54] Talking Paper, "Somalia Executive Committee Teleconference," 12 Nov 93, S-OADR, J-5 MEAF File.

[55] Msg, White House Situation Room to Joint Staff et al., 12 Nov 93, C; Memo, Richard Clarke to Somalia Exec Cmte, "Meeting on Tuesday, 16 March, 1:30 p.m.," 13 Nov 93, S-OADR; J-5 Issue Paper, "US Policy on Somalia," 15 Nov 93, S-OADR, J-5 MEAF File. Ironically, UNOSOM reached its peak strength in mid-November: 29,732 from twenty-nine nations. The Commission of Inquiry finally would produce an ambiguous report that distributed blame fairly widely.

[56] MG Carl F. Ernst, USA, 17 Jan 95 and LTG Thomas M. Montgomery, USA, 21 Jun 95 inteviewed by W. S. Poole; Msg, USLO Mogadishu 2530 to SecState, 17 Nov 93, C, J-5 MEAF File; MFR, Col Wahlquist to Amb Bogosian, n.d., C; Msg, USLO Mogadishu 2607 to SecState, 26 Nov 93, C. JTF Somalia was dissolved on 17 January.

[57] Memo, LTG Montgomery to BG Armstrong, 24 Apr 95, U.

[58] Early in January, on the advice of a UN legal adviser, Secretary General Boutros-Ghali ordered the last eight prisoners released.

[59] J-5 Talking Paper, "6 Dec 93 Somalia DC Mtg," 6 Dec 93, S-OADR; Form 136 J-4 Action 2121/430, 24 Nov 93, S-OADR, J-5 MEAF File.

[60] Msg, SecState 387511 to USLO Mogadishu, 29 Dec 93, C.

[61] USFORSOM After Action Report by MG Montgomery, Jun 94; J-3 Form 136, SJS 2121/ 439, "US Force Presence in Somalia after 31 March 1994," 27 Dec 93, C; Msgs, COMUS-FORSOMALIA to USCINCCENT, 131700Z and 241000Z Dec 93, C, J-5 MEAF File.

[62] Msg, USLO Mogadishu 261 to SecState, 6 Feb 94, C; Msg, Rabat 1271 to SecState et al., 8 Feb 94, C; Msg, USLO Mogadishu 395 to SecState, 21 Feb 94, C. A Malaysian officer, Lieutenant General Aboo, had replaced Lieutenant General Bir as Force Commander on 20 January. The Joint Staff opposed sending 258 trucks for the police, after learning that 267 Toyotas already had been made available from UN stocks at Mogadishu. On 9 December, the Somalia Executive Committee overrode the Joint Staff's objections. Memo, Dir, DSAA, to DJS, 10 Dec 93, U; Form 136, J-5 2121/426-1, 14 Dec 93, C.

[63] *Chicago Tribune*, 9 Feb 94, p. 7. Msg, USLO Mogadishu 540 to SecState, 8 Mar 94, C. Col Wahlquist's Notebook, 12 & 13 Mar 94.

Index

for UNOSOM: 3
for UNOSOM II: 33, 34, 35, 38, 39

Mahdi, Ali: 6, 16, 40, 64, 67
Malaysia: 57, 62, 87*n62*
Marine Amphibious Ready Groups
  off Mogadishu: 11, 16, 18, 19, 43, 54, 59, 86*n49*
  proposed use as Quick Reaction Force for UNOSOM: 33
Marine Corps, US
  forces for Somalia: 11, 24, 34–35, 66–67
  units stationed off Mogadishu: 11
Marine Division, 1st: 23–24
Marine Expeditionary Forces, 1st: 24–25, 26
Marine Expeditionary Unit: 24, 38, 46
McCaffrey, LTG Barry R., USA: 3, 20, 29, 42, 45, 47, 48, 52, 54, 56, 58–60, 77*n13*, *n14*, 81*n56*, 85*n41*
Meade, BG David C., USA: 23–24, 78*n21*
Medics: 27
Mediterranean Sky, MV: 65
Middle East–Africa Division: 82*n7*
  attitude toward State Department positions: 7, 9
  cost estimates: 77*n10*
  opposition to "points of security" strategy: 10
  papers drafted for the NSC Deputies Committee: 9, 44, 80*n51*
  PERT chart: 12, 18, 47, 51, 55
  proposals for US role: 17–18
  and proposed waiver of the Pressler Amendment: 31
  and UNOSOM II: 27, 28–29, 33–34, 64–65
Military Traffic Management Command: 24
Mogadishu, Somalia
  Aideed role in: 15, 41, 46, 47–48
  arrival of US forces in: 24–25, 26
  assessment of situation in: 19, 46, 63–64
  attacks on US soldiers in: 48
  Authorized Weapon Storage Sites: 41, 81*n1*, 85*n48*
  development of a police force in: 28

downing of US helicopters in: 56–57
foreign troops in: 11, 13, 15, 16, 24, 44, 50, 62–64, 79*n28*
Marines stationed near: 11
Pakistani soldiers in: 11, 13, 15, 16, 24, 79*n28*
proposals to send US troops to secure: 17
relief supplies for: 15, 16
UNOSOM II force used against Somalis: 44–45, 50
UNOSOM II mission in: 51
US assistance to UN officials in: 37, 46
US Liaison Office: 37, 45, 62, 63, 65–66, 67, 84*n27*
use of port at: 65
weapons in: 26, 29, 39–40, 43–44, 50, 81*n1*
Mombasa, Kenya: 8, 9, 24, 58, 65
Montgomery, MG Thomas M., USA: 37–38, 58, 63, 66, 80*n54*
  assessment of the situation: 41, 43–44, 51
  and control of the Quick Reaction Force: 38
  and downing of US helicopters: 56–57
  and efforts to capture Aideed: 45–46, 47, 56–58
  Joint Chiefs of Staff instructions to: 42
  and Joint Task Force Somalia: 61–62, 64, 86*n52*
  and requests for units and equipment: 43, 55–56, 81*n4*
  USCINCCENT instructions to: 61, 81*n6*
  and withdrawal from Somalia: 65–67
Moose, George: 52
Morgan, General Hersi: 6, 16–17
Morocco: 27, 28, 36, 41, 43, 44
Mountain Division, 10th: 24, 25, 56–57, 78*n21*, 81*n57*
Mubarak, Hosni: 47
Murdock, Clark: 55
Muslims: 41

Nairobi, Kenya: 67
Nation-building. *See also* Judicial system for Somalia; Police force for Somalia.

failure of effort: 51, 69
as UNOSOM mission: 22
UNOSOM II role in: 27, 34, 35, 39, 57, 65, 84*n26*
National Command Authority: 24, 61
National Intelligence Council: 35
National Security Council
  and allocation of airlift costs: 11
  Core Group: 26, 28–29
  Deputies Committee. *See* National Security Council Deputies Committee.
  Principals Committee: 35
  and proposed UN Security Council resolutions: 42
  staff. *See* National Security Council staff.
  tasking directives issued by: 58–59
  and UNOSOM II: 26–27
  and US transport for foreign troops: 13
National Security Council Deputies Committee
  and command of US troops: 18
  and creation of a national police force: 31, 49, 66
  and decentralization of UNOSOM II activities: 64–65
  discussions of policy options: 1, 19, 33, 34, 47, 48–49, 51, 54–55, 70
  and failure to adequately communicate policy adjustments: 4, 57–58
  inadequacies of policy development regarding Somalia: 4, 20, 70
  members: 7
  MEAF papers for: 9, 44
  and need for greater UN security presence: 13
  and need to capture Aideed: 3, 45–46, 47, 51
  and "points of security" strategy: 10, 11
  and political reconciliation in Somalia: 51
  and post-withdrawal aid to Somalia: 66
  and proposed shift to civilian carriers: 12, 13
  Somalia Coordination Committee: 86*n49*
  and UNOSOM II: 27, 37–38, 39
  and withdrawal of US troops from

Somalia: 39
National Security Council staff: 81*n2*
  and decentralization of UNOSOM II activities: 64–65
  and disarmament: 40
  effect of distractions on Somalia policy development: 51
  and effort to capture Aideed: 3, 46
Natsios, Andrew: 9, 10–11, 13, 16, 75*n9*
Navy, US
  and funding for Operation RESTORE HOPE: 32
  SEAL units: 24–25
  units for Operation RESTORE HOPE: 24
Nepal: 62
New Zealand: 30
Newton, LTC John, USAF: 7
Nigeria: 13, 17, 27, 30, 58, 62
Norway: 13

Oakley, Robert: 19–20, 23, 28, 31, 32, 35, 37, 39, 40, 59–60, 63, 64, 65
Oddur, Somalia: 25
Office of the Assistant Secretary of Defense (Regional Security Affairs): 52, 66
Office of the Secretary of Defense: 7, 46
Olympic Hotel: 56
Oman: 24
Operation DESERT SHIELD: 78*n25*
Operation PROVIDE COMFORT: 9
Operation PROVIDE RELIEF: 9–10, 75*n10*
Operation RESTORE HOPE: 23–26, 32–33, 39, 69, 78*n21*

Pakistan: 2, 3, 30, 36, 41–42, 57, 59, 62–63, 67
Pakistani troops
  Belgian troops in support of: 16–17
  June 1993 attack on: 2–3, 41
  in Mogadishu: 11, 13, 16–17, 24, 30–31, 41, 43–44, 57, 64, 79*n28*
  role of: 41
  for UNOSOM: 8, 11
  for UNOSOM II: 41, 44
  US support for: 8, 9, 10, 11, 24, 30–31

Perkins, Edward: 15, 16–17, 21–22
"Points of Security" strategy: 10, 12, 15
Police force for Somalia
    Clinton administration focus on: 48–49,
      60
    failure to establish: 37, 65, 66
    responsibility for creating: 31–32, 35, 39
    role of UNOSOM II in: 27, 34, 35, 57, 65
    UNITAF role in: 28, 31, 34
    as UNOSOM mission: 22
    US trainers for: 31–32
    US support for: 39, 49, 60, 65, 66, 87n62
Policy Coordinating Committee: 7, 8–9,
    10–11, 12, 15, 16, 55
Political goals, Joint Chiefs of Staff concern
    regarding the lack of: 1–2
Political reconciliation
    Addis Ababa accords: 31, 37
    agreement on transitional national
      council: 37
    "bottom up" approach to: 33–34, 35–36
    and decentralization of UNOSOM II
      activities: 64–65
    post-withdrawal failure of: 66–67
    as UNOSOM mission: 22, 33–34
    as UNOSOM II mission: 46, 51, 52,
      59–60
    US desire for UN to deal with: 18, 46
    as US mission: 61
Powell, General Colin L., USA: 80n51,
    84n31
    and Aideed: 45, 48, 70
    and foreign troops: 30
    and need for military intervention: 2,
      19–20, 69–70, 77n12
    and need to define political goals: 2, 19
    and UNITAF: 2, 23, 80n55, 81n56
    and UN Security Council Resolution
      837: 3, 81n2
    and UNOSOM II: 27, 30, 35, 37–38,
      41–42, 46, 49–50, 52, 54, 56
    and UNOSOM II planning: 43–44, 46,
      48
    and USCENTCOM mission: 23, 39, 40
    and use of SOF personnel: 45, 48, 70,
      83n18, 85n42
    warning orders to USCINCCENT: 17,

21–22
Presidential decision directives
    PDD-5: 54
    PDD-6: 38, 81n57
    PDD-25: 71
Pressler, Larry: 79n37
Pressler Amendment: 30–31
Program Evaluation and Review
    Techniques (PERT) chart: 12
    and interconnectedness of relief and
      political issues: 18, 51
    and UNOSOM II: 47, 51, 55
Public Law 103-50: 33

Quick Reaction Force
    command and control of: 38
    force protection role: 4, 52, 61
    Pakistani forces for: 67
    role of: 4, 52, 54, 56–57
    for UNOSOM: 3, 81n56, n57
    for UNOSOM II: 29, 33, 34, 35, 37–38,
      44, 48–49, 51, 52, 53, 56–57, 58–59,
      61–62
    US desire to limit the role of: 51, 52, 53
    US Marine Amphibious Ready Group
      as: 33
    US Marine Expeditionary unit as: 38
    use in efforts to capture Aideed: 45–46

"Radio Aideed": 41, 43
Ranger, USS: 21
Ranger Regiment, 75th: 48, 53, 58, 61
Relief supplies. *See also* Humanitarian
    operations.
    airlift of: 1, 7, 8, 9–10, 11, 12–13, 76n16,
      n18
    coordination of shipments of: 10
    cost estimates for airlift of: 7, 8, 11
    estimates of troops needed to protect:
      12–13, 15
    failure to reach the needy: 1, 16
    foreign donors: 39
    for Mogadishu: 15, 16
    "points of security" strategy to protect
      distribution of: 10, 12, 15
    security for distribution: 1, 21–23,
      61–62

Ryan, LTG Michael E., USAF: 47

Sahnoun, Mohammed: 6, 8, 13, 33
Saudi Arabia: 27, 28, 36, 62
Scowcroft, Brent: 21
Senegal: 15
Shalikashvili, General John M., USA: 61, 62, 65, 66, 67
Shinn, David: 46, 47, 69–70
Sicily: 24
Slocombe, Walter: 67
Somali clans, attachment to weapons: 2
Somali National Alliance militia: 41, 43, 44–45, 49, 63–64, 66, 82n8
Somali warlords, messages to regarding weapons: 26
Somalia
　agreement to establish a transitional national council: 37
　grants for local councils: 65
　justice system for: 49, 57, 66
　national police force. See Police force.
　post-withdrawal aid to: 66
　post-withdrawal deterioration of: 66–67
　proposed UNOSOM II role in the north of: 27–28, 30
　push for UN-sponsored trusteeship for: 15
　US refusal to deploy troops to northern areas of: 23, 26
Somalia Executive Committee: 60, 63, 65, 87n62
Somalia Working Group: 7, 8, 49, 55
South Korea: 54, 59
Spain: 24
Special Envoy to Somalia: 23. See also Gosende, Robert; Oakley, Robert.
Special Operations Forces, US
　Clinton position on the use of: 38
　command and control role in UNOSOM II operations: 43–44
　Howe's requests for: 43
　role in UNOSOM II operations: 43–44, 70
　units for Operation RESTORE HOPE: 24
　use of to capture Aideed: 3–4, 45–46,

48, 70, 82n10, 83n13, n18, 84n40
State, US Department of
　and Aideed: 3, 44, 45, 53
　and aircraft staging and refueling in foreign countries: 24
　and decentralization of UNOSOM II activities: 64–65
　and development of Somalia policy: 9
　failure to plan for contingencies: 51
　and Pakistani contributions: 30–31
　personnel in Somalia: 80n54
　and "points of security": 10
　and political reconciliation role for UNOSOM II: 53
　proposed use of US troops to guard food distribution facilities: 1
　and recruitment of foreign support for operations in Somalia: 35
　responsibility for airlift costs: 11, 13
　Security Council resolutions proposed by: 21, 22, 26–27, 80n46
　and US role in disarmament: 28
　and US transport for foreign troops: 13
Starvation
　brought under control: 39, 63
　efforts to avert: 1, 5, 6–10, 16, 39
Stettinius, Comdr. William, USN: 66
Sullivan, General Gordon R.: 56
Sweden: 30

Tanks
　Pakistani: 57, 58
　requests for: 4, 42–43, 55–56, 58, 63
Tarnoff, Peter: 46
Task Force Ranger: 48, 49, 50, 53, 56–57, 61, 83n18, 84n40
Terry, COL James P., USMC: 85n47
Time-Phased Force Deployment Data: 25–26
Timelines assumed for US military planning: 18, 21, 33
Transportation problems: 25–26
Tripoli, USS: 21, 78n15
Truck convoys: 10, 11, 12, 13
Tunisia: 30, 67
Turkey: 27, 28, 30, 36, 67

Unified Task Force (UNITAF)
command and control for foreign
troops: 28
costs of: 32–33
foreign troops for: 24, 28, 30–31, 32, 36,
80n55
mission: 2, 23
relationship with UNOSOM: 22, 23,
28–29
relationship with UNOSOM II: 27–28,
29, 30
role in disarmament: 26, 27–28, 39–40,
81n1
success of: 2, 39
transfer of responsibilities to UNOSOM
II: 2, 3, 28–29, 32–38, 39
troops for: 23, 28, 32, 33, 34–35
US logistic support for: 28, 80n55
United Arab Emirates: 27, 30, 62
United Kingdom: 46
United Nations
Contracts Committee: 61
credibility of peacekeeping operations:
15, 20, 33, 45, 63, 71
Department of Peacekeeping
Operations: 60
dependence on US logistical support: 39
failure to respond to Clinton's
announcement of a US withdrawal
deadline: 60
inability to support UN operations in
Somalia: 29–30, 32, 33, 35, 40
inadequacy of efforts in Somalia: 4, 5, 52
informed of US willingness to lead
military operations: 20
Joint Staff contingents sent to work at
Force Command headquarters: 29–30,
35
and logistic support contract: 60–61
"points of security" strategy: 10–11, 15
Secretariat's lack of clear plans for action
in Somalia: 16–17
understaffing of Force Command
headquarters: 40
US care to avoid indicating willingness
to fund missions: 12–13
US equipment leased to for use in

Somalia: 31
US funding for peacekeeping operations:
6–7
United Nations Charter
Chapter VI: 80n46
Chapter VII: 34, 36–37, 78n18, 80n46
United Nations Operations in Somalia
(UNOSOM)
command of: 22, 23
mission: 22, 23
Quick Reaction Force for: 3, 81n56, n57
relationship to UNITAF: 2, 3, 22, 23,
28–29
staffing of headquarters of: 3
troop strength: 8, 10, 21, 22, 23
troops comprising: 8, 23, 79n28
US logistic support for: 3
United Nations Operations in Somalia II
(UNOSOM II)
animosity of Somali factions toward: 41,
44–45, 50
assessment of threats facing: 41, 42, 63
command and control: 29, 30, 34, 35,
43–44, 49–50, 62
commander: 30, 34, 36–37, 66, 70–71,
87n62
decentralization of activities: 64–65
detainees: 86n58
and efforts to capture Aideed: 43–44,
50, 82n8
failure after withdrawal of US troops:
66–67, 70–71
failure to create an effective police force:
66, 70
foreign troops for: 30–31, 32, 36, 41, 43,
44, 47, 48, 54, 57, 59, 62–63, 86n55
headquarters: 64–66
Logistic Support Center: 66
nation-building role: 39, 69, 70, 84n26
need for a stronger UN mandate for:
26–27, 28, 35, 36–37, 80n46
need to integrate political, humanitarian,
and military roles: 46, 51, 53–54
and northern Somalia: 30
and political reconciliation: 51–52, 63
proposed US contributions to: 27, 29,
30, 32, 33, 34–35, 36, 37–38

UNOSOM II Strategy
Decision Points/ Follow On Actions

Humanitarian Actions

Food Lift
- inadequate → increase operatoins -press PVOs intn'l community
- adequate → Feed Population

Feed Population
- YES → Feed Population
- NO → improve distro network

Feed Population
- YES → Pop. Fed
- NO → reconsider options

Distribution Network

Food Production
- NO → market interventions -monetization livestock agriculture
- YES → Self Sufficiency

Self Sufficiency
- YES → Adequate Production
- NO → promote intn'l trade

Economic Rehab

Security Options

Port Security
- NO → UN guards local hires select alt. port
- YES → Food Security

Port Security
- YES → Food Security
- NO → change ROE

Food Security
- NO → increase guards -use force
- YES → Pop. Disarmed

Food Security
- YES →
- NO → consider mil. ops.

Pop. Disarmed
- YES → National Security Force
- NO → local police enforcement

Pop. Disarmed
- YES →
- NO → encamp militias

National Security Force

Peace & Stability

Political Actions

Local Ceasefires
- NO → conduct negotiations reward cooperation bolster Sahnoun
- YES → Regional Administration

Local Ceasefires
- YES →
- NO →

Regional Administration
- YES → National Reconciliation
- NO → invole third parties -regional treaties est. schools, police

National Reconciliation
- YES → Reestablish Basic Institutions
- NO → Regional Recon.

Regional Recon.
- YES →
- NO →

Reestablish Basic Institutions

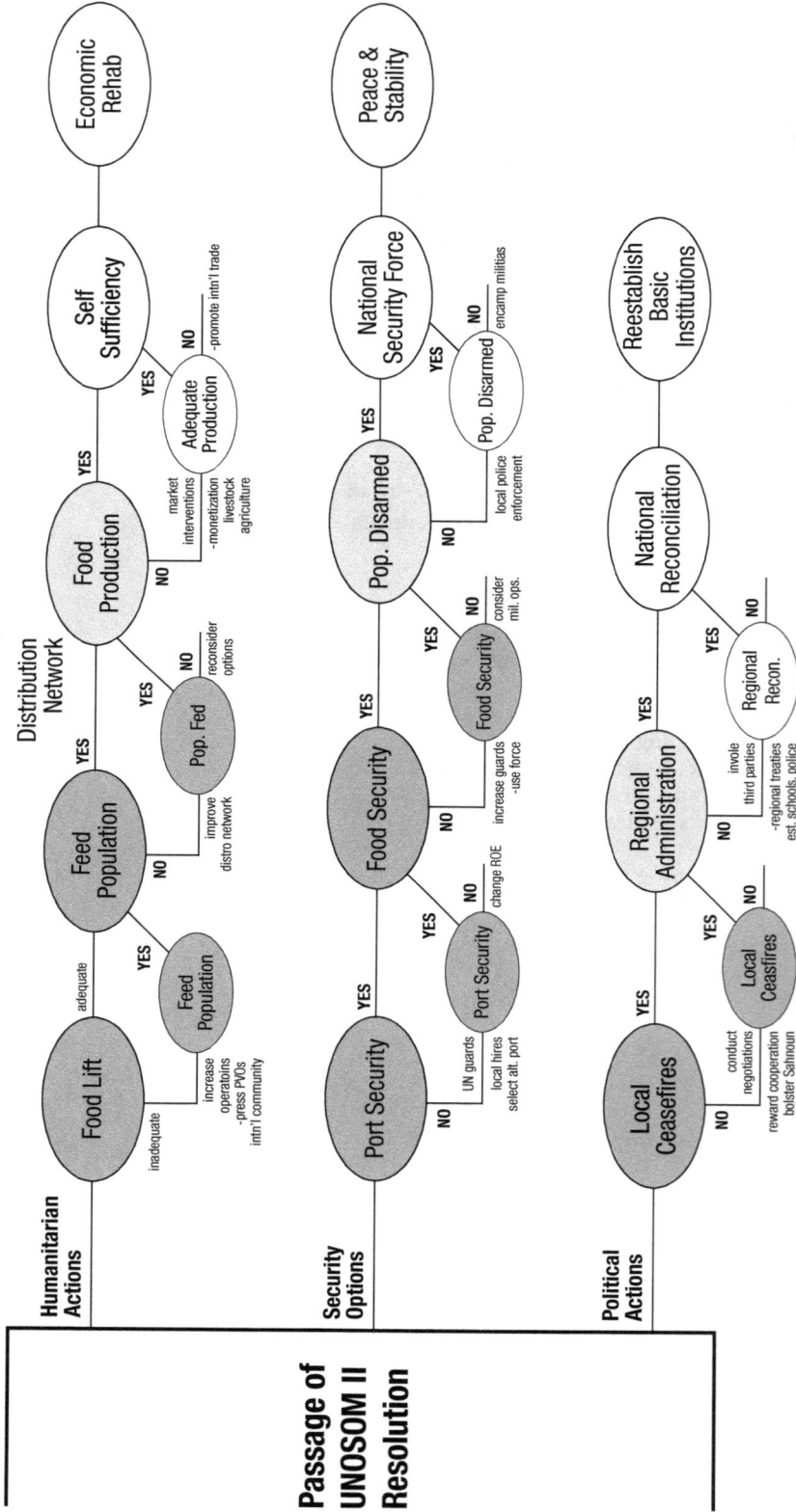

Passage of UNOSOM II Resolution

Accomplished

In Progress

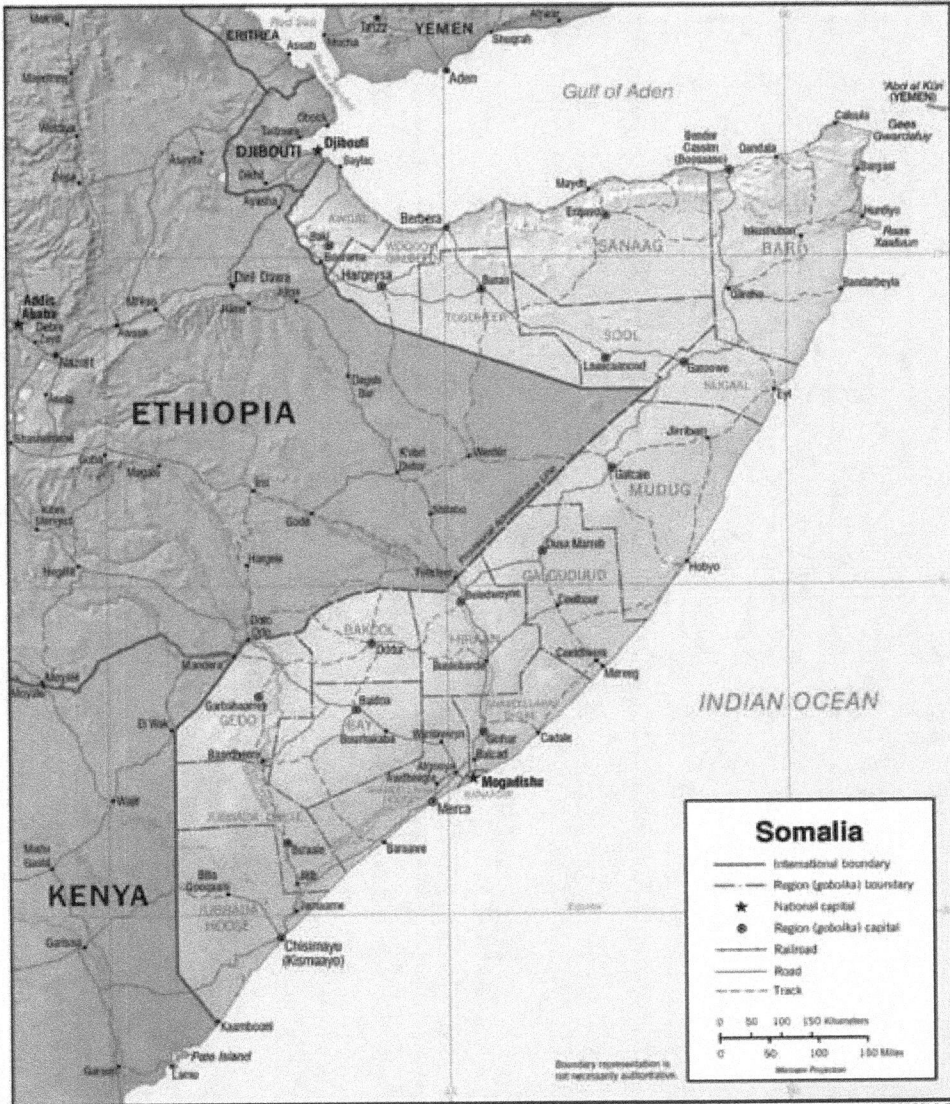